THE REAL LATIN QUARTER

By F. BERKELEY SMITH

WITH ILLUSTRATIONS BY THE AUTHOR
INTRODUCTION BY
F. HOPKINSON SMITH

Watchmaker Publishing
1901

Also from Watchmaker Publishing:
A Childhood in Brittany Eighty Years Ago
by Anne Douglas Sedgwick
ISBN 978-1603863018

CONTENTS

Introduction   7

Chapter

In the Rue Vaugirard   9

The Boulevard St. Michel   20

The "Bal Bullier"   35

Bal des Quat'z' Arts   44

"A Déjeuner at Lavenue's"   57

"At Marcel Legay's"   68

"Pochard"   76

The Luxembourg Gardens   88

"The Ragged Edge of the Quarter"   99

INTRODUCTION

ocher, drive to the rue Falguière"—this in my best restaurant French.

The man with the varnished hat shrugged his shoulders, and raised his eyebrows in doubt. He evidently had never heard of the rue Falguière. "Yes, rue Falguière, the old rue des Fourneaux," I continued.

Cabby's face broke out into a smile. "Ah, oui, oui, le Quartier Latin."

And it was at the end of this crooked street, through a lane that led into a half court flanked by a row of studio buildings, and up one pair of dingy waxed steps, that I found a door bearing the name of the author of the following pages—his visiting card impaled on a tack. He was in his shirt-sleeves—the thermometer stood at 90° outside—working at his desk, surrounded by half-finished sketches and manuscript.

The man himself I had met before—I had known him for years, in fact—but the surroundings were new to me. So too were his methods of work.

Nowadays when a man would write of the Siege of Peking or the relief of some South African town with the unpronounceable name, his habit is to rent a room on an up-town avenue, move in an inkstand and pad, and a collection of illustrated papers and encyclopedias. This writer on the rue Falguière chose a different plan. He would come back year after year, and study his subject and compile his impressions of the Quarter in the very atmosphere of the place itself; within a stone's throw of the Luxembourg Gardens and the Panthéon; near the cafés and the Bullier; next door, if you please, to the public laundry where his washerwoman pays a few sous for the privilege of pounding his clothes into holes.

It all seemed very real to me, as I sat beside him and watched him at work. The method delighted me. I have similar ideas myself about the value of his kind of study in out-door sketching, compared with the labored work of the studio, and I have most positive opinions regarding the quality which comes of it.

If then the pages which here follow have in them any of the true inwardness of the life they are meant to portray, it is due, I feel sure, as much to the attitude of the author toward his subject, as much to his ability to seize, retain, and express these instantaneous impressions, these flash pictures caught on the spot, as to any other merit which they may possess.

Nothing can be made really *real* without it.

F. HOPKINSON SMITH.
Paris, August, 1901.

CHAPTER I

❧

IN THE RUE VAUGIRARD

❧

Like a dry brook, its cobblestone bed zigzagging past quaint shops and cafés, the rue Vaugirard finds its way through the heart of the Latin Quarter.

It is only one in a score of other busy little streets that intersect the Quartier Latin; but as I live on the rue Vaugirard, or rather just beside it, up an alley and in the corner of a picturesque old courtyard leading to the "Lavoir Gabriel," a somewhat angelic name for a huge, barn-like structure reeking in suds and steam, and noisy with gossiping washerwomen who pay a few sous a day there for the privilege of doing their washing—and as my studio windows (the big one with the north light, and the other one a narrow slit reaching from the floor to the high ceiling for the taking in of the big canvases one sees at the Salon—which are never sold) overlook both alley and court, I can see the life and bustle below.

LAVOIR GABRIEL

This is not the Paris of Boulevards, ablaze with light and thronged with travelers of the world, nor of big hotels and chic restaurants without prices on the ménus. In the latter the maître d'hôtel makes a mental inventory of you when you arrive; and before you have reached your coffee and cigar, or before madame has buttoned her gloves, this well-shaved, dignified personage has passed sentence on you, and you pay according to whatever he thinks you cannot afford. I knew a fellow once who ordered a peach in winter at one of these smart taverns, and was obliged to wire home for money the next day.

In the Quartier Latin the price is always such an important factor that it is marked plainly, and often the garçon will remind you of the cost of the dish you select in case you have not read aright, for in this true Bohemia one's daily fortune is the one necessity so often lacking that any error in regard to its expenditure is a serious matter.

In one of the well-known restaurants—here celebrated as a rendezvous for artists—a waiter, as he took a certain millionaire's order for asparagus, said: "Does monsieur know that asparagus costs five francs?"

At all times of the day and most of the night the rue Vaugirard is busy. During the morning, push-carts loaded with red gooseberries, green peas, fresh sardines, and mackerel, their sides shining like silver, line the curb in front of the small shops. Diminutive donkeys, harnessed to picturesque two-wheeled carts piled high with vegetables, twitch their long ears and doze in the shady corners of the street. The gutters, flushed with clear water, flash in the sunlight. Baskets full of red roses and white carnations, at a few sous the armful, brighten the cool shade of the alleys leading to courtyards of wild gardens, many of which are filled with odd collections of sculpture discarded from the ateliers.

Old women in linen caps and girls in felt slippers and leather-covered sabots, market baskets on arm, gossip in groups or hurry along the narrow sidewalk, stopping at the butcher's or the baker's to buy the déjeuner. Should you breakfast in your studio and do your own marketing, you will meet with enough politeness in the buying of a paté, an artichoke, and a bottle of vin ordinaire, to supply a court welcoming a distinguished guest.

Politeness is second nature to the Parisian—it is the key to one's daily life here, the oil that makes this finesse of civilization run smoothly.

"Bonjour, madame!" says the well-to-do proprietor of the tobacco-shop and café to an old woman buying a sou's worth of snuff.

"Bonjour, monsieur," replies the woman with a nod.

"Merci, madame," continues the fat patron as he drops the sou into his till.

"Merci, monsieur—merci!" and she secretes the package in her netted reticule, and hobbles out into the sunny street, while the patron attends to the wants of three draymen who have clambered down from their heavy carts for a friendly chat and a little vermouth. A polished zinc bar runs the length of the low-ceilinged room; a narrow, winding stairway in one corner leads to the living apartments above. Behind the bar shine three well-polished square mirrors, and ranged in front of these, each in its zinc rack, are the favorite beverages of the Quarter—anisette, absinthe, menthe, grenadine—each in zinc-stoppered bottles, like the ones in the barber-shops.

At the end of the little bar a cocher is having his morning tipple, the black brim of his yellow glazed hat resting on his coarse red ears. He is in his shirt-sleeves; coat slung over his shoulder, and whip in hand, he is on the way to get his horse and voiture for the day. To be even a cocher in Paris is considered a profession. If he dines at six-thirty and you hail him to take you as he rattles past, he will make his brief apologies to you without slackening his pace, and go on to his plat du jour and bottle of wine at his favorite rendezvous, dedicated to "The Faithful Cocher." An hour later he emerges, well fed, revives his knee-sprung horse, lights a fresh cigarette, cracks his whip like a package of torpedoes, and goes clattering off in search of a customer.

The shops along the rue Vaugirard are- marvels of neatness. The butcher-shop, with its red front, is iron-barred like the lion's cage in the circus. Inside the cage are some choice specimens of filets, rounds of beef, death-masks of departed calves, cutlets, and chops in paper pantalettes. On each article is placed a brass sign with the current price thereon.

In Paris nothing is wasted. A placard outside the butcher's announces an "Occasion" consisting of a mule and a donkey, both of guaranteed "première qualité." And the butcher! A thick-set, powerfully built fellow, with blue-black hair, curly like a bull's and shining in pomade, with fierce mustache of the same dye, waxed to two formidable points like skewers. Dangling over his white apron, and suspended by a heavy chain about his waist, he carries the long steel spike which sharpens his knives. All this paraphernalia gives him a very fierce appearance, like the executioner in the play; but you will find him a mild, kindly man after all, who takes his absinthe slowly, with a fund of good humor after his day's work, and his family to Vincennes on Sundays.

The windows, too, of these little shops are studies in decoration. If it happens to be a problem in eggs, cheese, butter, and milk, all these are arranged artistically with fresh grape-leaves between the white rows of milk bottles and under the cheese; often the leaves form a nest for the white eggs (the fresh ones)—the hard-boiled ones are dyed a bright crimson. There are china hearts, too, filled with "Double Cream," and cream in little brown pots; Roquefort cheese and Camembert, Isijny, and Pont Levéque, and chopped spinach.

Delicatessen shops display galantines of chicken, the windows banked with shining cans of sardines and herrings from Dieppe; liver patés and creations in jelly; tiny sausages of doubtful stuffing, and occasional yellow ones like the odd fire-cracker of the pack.

Grocery shops, their interiors resembling the toy ones of our childhood, are brightened with cones of snowy sugar in blue paper jackets. The wooden drawers- filled with spices. Here, too, one can get an excellent light wine for eight sous the bottle.

As the day begins, the early morning cries drift up from the street. At six the fishwomen with their push-carts go their rounds, each singing the beauties of her wares. "Voilà les beaux maquereaux!" chants the sturdy vendor, her sabots clacking over the cobbles as she pushes the cart or stops and weighs a few sous' worth of fish to a passing purchaser.

The goat-boy, piping his oboe-like air, passes, the goats scrambling ahead alert to steal a carrot or a bite of cabbage from the nearest cart. And when these have passed, the little orgue de Barbarie plays its repertoire of quadrilles and waltzes under your window. It is a very sweet-toned organ, this little orgue de Barbarie, with a plaintive, apologetic tone, and a flute obbligato that would do credit to many a small orchestra. I know this small organ well—an old friend on dreary mornings, putting the laziest riser in a good humor for the day. The tunes are never changed,- but they are all inoffensive and many of them pretty, and to the shrunken old man who grinds them out daily they are no doubt by this time all alike.

It is growing late and time for one's coffee. The little tobacco-shop and café around the corner I find an excellent place for café au lait. The coffee is delicious and made when one chooses to arrive, not stewed like soup, iridescent in color, and bitter with chicory, as one finds it in many of the small French hotels. Two crescents, flaky and hot from the bakery next door, and three generous pats of unsalted butter, complete this morning repast, and all for the modest sum of twelve sous, with three sous to the garçon who serves you, with which he is well pleased.

I have forgotten a companionable cat who each morning takes her seat on the long leather settee beside me and shares my crescents. The cats are considered important members of nearly every family in the Quarter. Big yellow and gray Angoras, small, alert tortoise-shell ones, tiger-like and of plainer breed and more intelligence, bask in the doorways or sleep on the marble-topped tables of the cafés.

"Qu'est-ce que tu veux, ma pauvre Mimi?" condoles Céleste, as she approaches the family feline.

"Mimi" stretches her full length, extending and retracting her claws, rolls on her back, turns her big yellow eyes to Céleste and mews. The next moment she is picked up and carried back into the house like a stray child.

At noon the streets seem deserted, except for the sound of occasional laughter and the rattle of dishes coming from the smaller restaurants as one passes. At this hour these places are full of workmen in white and blue blouses, and young girls from the neighboring factories. They are all laughing and talking together. A big fellow in a blue gingham blouse attempts to kiss the little milliner opposite him at table; she evades him, and, screaming with laughter, picks up her skirts and darts out of the restaurant and down the street, the big fellow close on her dainty heels. A second later he has overtaken her, and picking her up bodily in his strong arms carries her back to her seat, where he places her in her chair, the little milliner by this time quite out of breath with laughter and quite happy. This little episode affords plenty of amusement to the rest of the crowd; they wildly applaud the good-humored captor, who orders another litre of red wine for those present, and everyone is merry.

The Parisian takes his hour for déjeuner, no matter what awaits him. It is the hour when lovers meet, too. Edmond, working in the atelier for the reproduction of Louis XVI furniture, meets Louise coming from her work on babies' caps in the rue des Saints-Pères at precisely twelve-ten on the corner of the rue Vaugirard and the Boulevard Montparnasse. Louise comes without her hat, her hair in an adorable coiffure, as neatly arranged as a Geisha's, her skirt held tightly to her hips, disclosing her small feet in low slippers. There is a golden rule, I believe, in the French catechism which says: "It is better, child, that thy hair be neatly dressed than that thou shouldst have a whole frock." And so Louise is content. The two breakfast on a ragoût and a bottle of wine while they talk of going on Sunday to St. Cloud for the day—and so they must be economical this week. Yes, they will surely go to St. Cloud and spend all day in the woods. It is the second Sunday in the month, and the fountains will be playing. They will take their déjeuner with them. Louise will, of course, see to this, and Edmond will bring cigarettes enough for two, and the wine. Then, when the stars are out, they will take one of the "bateaux mouches" back to Paris.

Dear Paris—the Paris of youth, of love, and of romance!

The pulse of the Quarter begins really to beat at 6 P.M. At this hour the streets are alive with throngs of workmen—after their day's work, seeking their favorite cafés to enjoy their apéritifs with their comrades—and women hurrying back from their work, many to their homes and children, buying the dinner en route.

Henriette, who sews all day at one of the fashionable dressmakers' in the rue de la Paix, trips along over the Pont Neuf to her small room in the Quarter to put on her best dress and white kid slippers, for it is Bullier night and she is going to the ball with two friends of her cousin.

In the twilight, and from my studio window the swallows, like black cinders against the yellow sky, dart and swoop above the forest of chimney-pots and tiled and gabled roofs.

It is the hour to dine, and with this thought uppermost in every one's mind studio doors are slammed and night-keys tucked in pockets. And arm in arm the poet and the artist swing along to that evening Mecca of good Bohemians—the Boulevard St. Michel.

CHAPTER II

❧

THE BOULEVARD ST. MICHEL

❧

ROM the Place St. Michel, this ever gay and crowded boulevard ascends a long incline, up which the tired horses tug at the traces of the fiacres, and the big double-decked steam trams crawl, until they reach the Luxembourg Gardens,—and so on a level road as far as the Place de l'Observatoire. Within this length lies the life of the "Boul' Miche."

Nearly every highway has its popular side, and on the "Boul' Miche" it is the left one, coming up from the Seine. Here are the cafés, and from 5 P.M. until long past midnight, the life of the Quartier pours by them—students, soldiers, families, poets, artists, sculptors, wives, and sweethearts; bicycle girls, the modern grisette, the shop girl, and the model; fakirs, beggars, and vagrants. Yet the word vagrant is a misnomer in this city, where economy has reached a finesse that is marvelous. That fellow, in filth and rags, shuffling along, his eyes scrutinizing, like a hungry rat, every nook and corner under the café tables on the terrace, carries a stick spiked with a pin. The next instant, he has raked the butt of your discarded cigarette from beneath your feet with the dexterity of a croupier. The butt he adds to the collection in his filthy pocket, and shuffles on to the next café. It will go so far at least toward paying for his absinthe. He is hungry, but it is the absinthe for which he is working. He is a "marchand de mégots"; it is his profession.

TERRACE TAVERNE DU PANTHÉON

One finds every type of restaurant, tavern, and café along the "Boul' Miche." There are small restaurants whose plat du jour might be traced to some faithful steed finding a final oblivion in a brown sauce and onions—an important item in a course dinner, to be had with wine included for one franc fifty. There are brasseries too, gloomy by day and brilliant by night (dispensing good Munich beer in two shades, and German and French food), whose rich interiors in carved black oak, imitation gobelin, and stained glass are never half illumined until the lights are lit.

A "TYPE"

All day, when the sun blazes, and the awnings are down, sheltering those chatting on the terrace, the interiors of these brasseries appear dark and cavernous.

The clientèle is somber too, and in keeping with the place; silent poets, long haired, pale, and always writing; serious-minded lawyers, lunching alone, and fat merchants who eat and drink methodically.

Then there are bizarre cafés, like the d'Harcourt, crowded at night with noisy women tawdry in ostrich plumes, cheap feather boas, and much rouge. The d'Harcourt at midnight is ablaze with light, but the crowd is common and you move on up the boulevard under the trees, past the shops full of Quartier fashions—velvet coats, with standing collars buttoning close under the chin; flamboyant black silk scarfs tied in a huge bow;

queer broad-brimmed, black hats without which no "types" wardrobe is complete.

On the corner facing the square, and opposite the Luxembourg gate, is the Taverne du Panthéon. This is the most brilliant café and restaurant of the Quarter, forming a V with its long terrace, at the corner of the boulevard and the rue Soufflot, at the head of which towers the superb dome of the Panthéon.

It is 6 P.M. and the terrace, four rows deep with little round tables, is rapidly filling. The white-aproned garçons are hurrying about or squeezing past your table, as they take the various orders.

"Un demi! un!" shouts the garçon.

"Deux pernod nature, deux!" cries another, and presently the "Omnibus" in his black apron hurries to your table, holding between his knuckles, by their necks, half a dozen bottles of different apéritifs, for it is he who fills your glass.

ALONG THE "BOUL' MICHE"

It is the custom to do most of one's correspondence in these cafés. The garçon brings you a portfolio containing note-paper, a bottle of violet ink, an impossible pen that spatters, and a sheet of pink blotting-paper that does not absorb. With these and your apéritif, the place is yours as long as you choose to remain. No one will ask you to "move on" or pay the slightest attention to you.

Should you happen to be a cannibal chief from the South Seas, and dine in a green silk high hat and a necklace of your latest captive's teeth, you would occasion a passing glance perhaps, but you would not be a sensation.

Céleste would say to Henriette:

"Regarde ça, Henriette! est-il drôle, ce sauvage?"

And Henriette would reply quite assuringly:

"Eh bien quoi! c'est pas si extraordinaire, il est peut-être de Madagascar; il y en a beaucoup à Paris maintenant."

There is no phase of character, or eccentricity of dress, that Paris has not seen.

Nor will your waiter polish off the marble top of your table, with the hope that your ordinary sensibility will suggest another drink. It would be beneath his professional dignity as a good garçon de café. The two sous you have given him as a pourboire, he is well satisfied with, and expresses his contentment in a "merci, monsieur, merci," the final syllable ending in a little hiss, prolonged in proportion to his satisfaction. After this just formality, you will find him ready to see the point of a joke or discuss the current topics of the day. He is intelligent, independent, very polite, but never servile.

It is difficult now to find a vacant chair on the long terrace. A group of students are having a "Pernod," after a long day's work at the atelier. They finish their absinthe and then, arm in arm, start off to Madame Poivret's for dinner. It is cheap there; besides, the little "boîte," with its dingy room and sawdust floor, is a favorite haunt of theirs, and the good old lady, with her credit slate, a friendly refuge in time of need.

At your left sits a girl in bicycle bloomers, yellow-tanned shoes, and short black socks pulled up snug to her sunburned calves. She has just ridden in from the Bois de Boulogne, and has scorched half the way back to meet her "officier" in pale blue. The two are deep in conversation. Farther on are four older men, accompanied by a pale, sweet-faced woman of thirty, her blue-black hair brought in a bandeau over her dainty ears. She is the model of the gray-haired man on the left, a man of perhaps fifty, with kindly intelligent eyes and strong, nervous, expressive hands—hands that know how to model a colossal Greek war-horse, plunging in battle, or create a nymph scarcely a foot high out of a lump of clay, so charmingly that the French

Government has not only bought the nymph, but given him a little red ribbon for his pains.

He is telling the others of a spot he knows in Normandy, where one can paint—full of quaint farm-houses, with thatched roofs; picturesque roadsides, rich in foliage; bright waving fields, and cool green woods, and purling streams; quaint gardens, choked with lavender and roses and hollyhocks—and all this fair land running to the white sand of the beach, with the blue sea beyond. He will write to old Père Jaqueline that they are all coming—it is just the place in which to pose a model "en plein air,"—and Suzanne, his model, being a Normande herself, grows enthusiastic at the thought of going down again to the sea. Long before she became a Parisienne, and when her beautiful hair was a tangled shock of curls, she used to go out in the big boats, with the fisherwomen—barefooted, brown, and happy. She tells them of those good days, and then they all go into the Taverne to dine, filled with the idea of the new trip, and dreaming of dinners under the trees, of "Tripes à la mode de Caen," Normandy cider, and a lot of new sketches besides.

Already the tables within are well filled. The long room, with its newer annex, is as brilliant as a jewel box—the walls rich in tiled panels suggesting the life of the Quarter, the woodwork in gold and light oak, the big panels of the rich gold ceiling exquisitely painted.

At one of the tables two very chic young women are dining with a young Frenchman, his hair and dress in close imitation of the Duc d'Orleans. These poses in dress are not uncommon.

A strikingly pretty woman, in a scarlet-spangled gown as red as her lips, is dining with a well-built, soldierly-looking man in black; they sit side by side as is the custom here.

The woman reminds one of a red lizard—a salamander—her "svelte" body seemingly boneless in its gown of clinging scales. Her hair is purple-black and freshly onduléd; her skin as white as ivory. She has the habit of throwing back her small, well-posed head, while under their delicately penciled lids her gray eyes take in the room at a glance.

She is not of the Quarter, but the Taverne du Panthéon is a refuge for her at times, when she grows tired of Paillard's and Maxim's and her quarreling retinue.

"Let them howl on the other bank of the Seine," says this empress of the half-world to herself, "I dine with Raoul where I please."

And now one glittering, red arm with its small, heavily-jeweled hand glides toward Raoul's open cigarette case, and in withdrawing a cigarette she presses for a moment his big, strong hand as he holds near her polished nails the flaming match.

ALONG THE SEINE

Her companion watches her as she smokes and talks—now and then he leans closer to her, squaring his broad shoulders and bending lower his strong, determined face, as he listens to her,—

half-amused, replying to her questions leisurely, in short, crisp sentences. Suddenly she stamps one little foot savagely under the table, and, clenching her jeweled hands, breathes heavily. She is trembling with rage; the man at her side hunches his great shoulders, flicks the ashes from his cigarette, looks at her keenly for a moment, and then smiles. In a moment she is herself again, almost penitent; this little savage, half Roumanian, half Russian, has never known what it was to be ruled! She has seen men grow white when she has stamped her little foot, but this big Raoul, whom she loves—who once held a garrison with a handful of men—he does not tremble! she loves him for his devil-me-care indifference—and he enjoys her temper.

But the salamander remembers there are some whom she dominated, until they groveled like slaves at her feet; even the great Russian nobleman turned pale when she dictated to him archly and with the voice of an angel the price of his freedom.

"Poor fool! he shot himself the next day," mused the salamander.

Yes, and even the adamant old banker in Paris, crabbed, stern, unrelenting to his debtors—shivered in his boots and ended in signing away half his fortune to her, and moved his family into a permanent chateau in the country, where he keeps himself busy with his shooting and his books.

As it grows late, the taverne becomes more and more animated.

Everyone is talking and having a good time. The room is bewildering in gay color, the hum of conversation is everywhere, and as there is a corresponding row of tables across the low, narrow room, friendly greetings and often conversations are kept up from one side to the other. The dinner, as it progresses, assumes the air of a big family party of good bohemians. The French do not bring their misery with them to the table. To dine is to enjoy oneself to the utmost; in fact the French people cover their disappointment, sadness, annoyances, great or petty troubles, under a masque of "blague," and have such an innate dislike of sympathy or ridicule that they avoid it by turning everything into "blague."

This veneer is misleading, for at heart the French are sad. Not to speak of their inmost feelings does not, on the other hand, prevent them at times from being most confidential. Often, the merest exchange of courtesies between those sharing the same compartment in a train, or a seat on a "bus," seems to be a sufficient introduction for your neighbor to tell you where he comes from, where he is going, whether he is married or single, whom his daughter married, and what regiment his son is in. These little confidences often end in his offering you half his bottle of wine and extending to you his cigarettes.

LES BEAUX MAQUEREAUX

If you have finished dinner, you go out on the terrace for your coffee. The fakirs are passing up and down in front, selling their wares—little rabbits, wonderfully lifelike, that can jump along your table and sit on their hind legs, and wag their ears; toy snakes; small leaden pigs for good luck; and novelties of every description. Here one sees women with baskets of écrivisse boiled scarlet; an acrobat tumbles on the pavement, and two men and a girl, as a marine, a soldier, and a vivandière, in silvered faces and suits, pose in melodramatic attitudes. The vivandière is rescued alternately from a speedy death by the marine and the soldier.

Presently a little old woman approaches, shriveled and smiling, in her faded furbelows now in rags. She sings in a piping voice and executes between the verses a tottering pas seul, her eyes ever smiling, as if she still saw over the glare of the footlights, in the haze beyond, the vast audience of by-gone days; smiling as if she still heard the big orchestra and saw the leader with his vibrant baton, watching her every movement. She is over seventy now, and was once a premier danseuse at the opera.

But you have not seen all of the Taverne du Panthéon yet. There is an "American Bar" downstairs; at least, so the sign reads at the top of a narrow stairway leading to a small, tavern-like room, with a sawdust floor, heavy deal tables, and wooden stools. In front of the bar are high stools that one climbs up on and has a lukewarm whisky soda, next to Yvonne and Marcelle, who are both singing the latest catch of the day at the top of their lungs, until they are howled at to keep still or are lifted bodily off their high stools by the big fellow in the "type" hat, who has just come in.

MOTHER AND DAUGHTER

Before a long table at one end of the room is the crowd of American students singing in a chorus. The table is full now, for many have come from dinners at other cafés to join them. At one end, and acting as interlocutor for this impromptu minstrel show, presides one of the best fellows in the world. He rises solemnly, his genial round face wreathed in a subtle smile, and announces that he will sing, by earnest request, that popular ballad, "'Twas Summer and the Little Birds were Singing in the Trees."

There are some especially fine "barber chords" in this popular ditty, and the words are so touching that it is repeated over and over again. Then it is sung softly like the farmhand quartettes do in the rural melodrama outside the old homestead in harvest time. Oh! I tell you it's a truly rural octette. Listen to that exhibition bass voice of Jimmy Sands and that wandering tenor of Tommy Whiteing, and as the last chord dies away (over the fields presumably) a shout goes up:

"How's that?"

"Out of sight," comes the general verdict from the crowd, and bang go a dozen beer glasses in unison on the heavy table.

"Oh, que c'est beau!" cries Mimi, leading the successful chorus in a new vocal number with Edmond's walking-stick; but this time it is a French song and the whole room is singing it, including our old friend, Monsieur Frank, the barkeeper, who is mixing one of his famous concoctions which are never twice quite alike, but are better than if they were.

The harmonic beauties of "'Twas Summer and the Little Birds were Singing in the Trees" are still inexhausted, but it sadly needs a piano accompaniment—with this it would be perfect; and so the whole crowd, including Yvonne, and Céleste, and Marcelle, and the two Frenchmen, and the girl in the bicycle clothes, start for Jack Thompson's studio in the rue des Fourneaux, where there is a piano that, even if the candles in the little Louis XVI brackets do burn low and spill down the keys, and the punch rusts the strings, it will still retain that beautiful, rich tone that every French upright, at seven francs a month, possesses.

CHAPTER III

❧

THE "BAL BULLIER"

❧

There are all types of "bals" in Paris. Over in Montmartre, on the Place Blanche, is the well-known "Moulin Rouge," a place suggestive, to those who have never seen it, of the quintessence of Parisian devil-me-care gaiety. You expect it to be like those clever pen-and-ink drawings of Grevin's, of the old Jardin Mabille in its palmiest days, brilliant with lights and beautiful women extravagantly gowned and bejeweled. You expect to see Frenchmen, too, in pot-hats, crowding in a circle about Fifine, who is dancing some mad can-can, half hidden in a swirl of point lace, her small, polished boots alternately poised above her dainty head. And when she has finished, you expect her to be carried off to supper at the Maison Dorée by the big, fierce-looking Russian who has been watching her, and whose victoria, with its spanking team—black and glossy as satin—champing their silver bits outside, awaiting her pleasure.

But in all these anticipations you will be disappointed, for the famous Jardin Mabille is no more, and the ground where it once stood in the Champs Elysées is now built up with private residences. Fifine is gone, too—years ago—and most of the old gentlemen in pot-hats who used to watch her are buried or about to be. Few Frenchmen ever go to the "Moulin Rouge," but every American does on his first night in Paris, and emerges with enough cab fare to return him to his hotel, where he arrives with the positive conviction that the red mill, with its slowly revolving sails, lurid in crimson lights, was constructed especially for him. He remembers, too, his first impressions of Paris that very morning as his train rolled into the Gare St. Lazare. His aunt could wait until tomorrow to see the tomb of Napoleon, but he would see the "Moulin Rouge" first, and to be in ample time ordered dinner early in his expensive, morgue-like hotel.

I remember once, a few hours after my arrival in Paris, walking up the long hill to the Place Blanche at 2 P.M., under a blazing July sun, to see if they did not give a matinée at the "Moulin Rouge." The place was closed, it is needless to say, and the policeman I found pacing his beat outside, when I asked him what day they gave a matinée, put his thumbs in his sword belt, looked at me quizzically for a moment, and then roared. The "Moulin Rouge" is in full blast every night; in the day-time it is being aired.

Farther up in Montmartre, up a steep, cobbly hill, past quaint little shops and cafés, the hill becoming so steep that your cab horse finally refuses to climb further, and you get out and walk up to the "Moulin de la Galette." You find it a far different type of ball from the "Moulin Rouge," for it is not made for the stranger, and its clientèle is composed of the rougher element of that quarter.

A few years ago the "Galette" was not the safest of places for a stranger to go to alone. Since then, however, this ancient granary and mill, that has served as a ball-room for so many years, has undergone a radical change in management; but it is still a cliquey place, full of a lot of habitués who regard a stranger as an intruder. Should you by accident step on Marcelle's dress or jostle her villainous-looking escort, you will be apt to get into a row, beginning with a mode of attack you are possibly ignorant of, for these "maquereaux" fight with their feet, having developed this "manly art" of self-defense to a point of dexterity more to be evaded than admired. And while Marcelle's escort, with a swinging kick, smashes your nose with his heel, his pals will take the opportunity to kick you in the back.

So, if you go to the "Galette," go with a Parisian or some of the students of the Quarter; but if you must go alone—keep your eyes on the band. It is a good band, too, and its chef d'orchestre, besides being a clever musical director, is a popular composer as well.

Go out from the ball-room into the tiny garden and up the ladder-like stairs to the rock above, crowned with the old windmill, and look over the iron railing. Far below you, swimming in a faint mist under the summer stars, all Paris lies glittering at your feet.

You will find the "Bal Bullier" of the Latin Quarter far different from the "bals" of Montmartre. It forms, with its "grand fête" on Thursday nights, a sort of social event of the week in this Quarter of Bohemians, just as the Friday afternoon promenade does in the Luxembourg garden.

If you dine at the Taverne du Panthéon on a Thursday night you will find that the taverne is half deserted by 10 o'clock, and that everyone is leaving and walking up the "Boul' Miche" toward the "Bullier." Follow them, and as you reach the place l'Observatoire, and turn a sharp corner to the left, you will see the façade of this famous ball, illumined by a sizzling blue electric light over the entrance.

The façade, with its colored bas-reliefs of students and grisettes, reminds one of the proscenium of a toy theater. Back of this shallow wall bristle the tops of the trees in the garden adjoining the big ball-room, both of which are below the level of the street and are reached by a broad wooden stairway.

The "Bal Bullier" was founded in 1847; previous to this there existed the "Closerie des Lilas" on the Boulevard Montparnasse. You pass along with the line of waiting poets and artists, buy a green ticket for two francs at the little cubby-hole of a box-office, are divested of your stick by one of half a dozen white-capped matrons at the vestiaire, hand your ticket to an elderly gentleman in a silk hat and funereal clothes, at the top of the stairway sentineled by a guard of two soldiers, and the next instant you see the ball in full swing below you.

There is nothing disappointing about the "Bal Bullier." It is all you expected it to be, and more, too. Below you is a veritable whirlpool of girls and students—a vast sea of heads, and a dazzling display of colors and lights and animation. Little shrieks and screams fill your ears, as the orchestra crashes into the last page of a gallop, quickening the pace until Yvonne's little feet slip and her cheeks glow, and her eyes grow bright, and half her pretty golden hair gets smashed over her impudent little nose. Then the gallop is brought up with a quick finish.

"Bis! Bis! Bis! Encore!" comes from every quarter of the big room, and the conductor, with his traditional good-nature, begins again. He knows it is wiser to humor them, and off they go again, still faster, until all are out of breath and rush into the garden for a breath of cool air and a "citron glacé."

And what a pretty garden it is!—full of beautiful trees and dotted with round iron tables, and laid out in white gravel walks, the garden sloping gently back to a fountain, and a grotto and an artificial cascade all in one, with a figure of Venus in the center, over which the water splashes and trickles. There is a green lattice proscenium, too, surrounding the fountain, illuminated with colored lights and outlined in tiny flames of gas, and grotto-like alcoves circling the garden, each with a table and room for two. The ball-room from the garden presents a brilliant contrast, as one looks down upon it from under the trees.

But the orchestra has given its signal—a short bugle call announcing a quadrille; and those in the garden are running down into the ball-room to hunt up their partners.

The "Bullier" orchestra will interest you; they play with a snap and fire and a tempo that is irresistible. They have played together so long that they have become known as the best of all the bal orchestras.

The leader, too, is interesting—tall and gaunt, with wild, deep-sunken eyes resembling those of an old eagle. Now and then he turns his head slowly as he leads, and rests these keen, penetrating orbs on the sea of dancers below him. Then, with baton raised above his head, he brings his orchestra into the wild finale of the quadrille—piccolos and clarinets, cymbals, bass viols, and violins—all in one mad race to the end, but so well trained that not a note is lost in the scramble—and they finish under the wire to a man, amid cheers from Mimi and Céleste and "encores" and "bis's" from everyone else who has breath enough left to shout with.

A TYPE OF THE QUARTER
By Helleu.—Estampe Moderne

Often after an annual dinner of one of the ateliers, the entire body of students will march into the "Bullier," three hundred strong, and take a good-natured possession of the place. There have been some serious demonstrations in the Quarter by the students, who can form a small army when combined. But as a rule you will find them a good-natured lot of fellows, who are out for all the humor and fun they can create at the least expense.

But in June, 1893, a serious demonstration by the students occurred, for these students can fight as well as dance. Senator Beranger, having read one morning in the "Courrier Français" an account of the revelry and nudity of several of the best-known models of the Quarter at the "Quat'z' Arts" ball, brought a charge against the organizers of the ball, and several of the models, whose beauty unadorned had made them conspicuous on this most festive occasion. At the ensuing trial, several celebrated beauties and idols of the Latin Quarter were convicted and sentenced to a short term of imprisonment, and fined a hundred francs each. These sentences were, however, remitted, but the majority of the students would not have it thus, and wanted further satisfaction. A mass meeting was held by them in the Place de la Sorbonne. The police were in force there to stop any disturbance, and up to 10 o'clock at night the crowd was held in control.

It was a warm June night, and every student in the Quarter was keyed to a high state of excitement. Finally a great crowd of students formed in front of the Café d'Harcourt, opposite the Sorbonne; things were at fever heat; the police became rough; and in the row that ensued, somebody hurled one of the heavy stone match-safes from a café table at one of the policemen, who in his excitement picked it up and hurled it back into the crowd. It struck and injured fatally an innocent outsider, who was taken to the Charity Hospital, in the rue Jacob, and died there.

On the following Monday another mass meeting of students was held in the Place de la Sorbonne, who, after the meeting, formed in a body and marched to the Chamber of Deputies, crying: "Conspuez Dupuy," who was then president of the Chamber. A number of deputies came out on the portico and the terrace, and smilingly reviewed the demonstration, while the students hurled their anathemas at them, the leaders and men in the front rank of this howling mob trying to climb over the high railing in front of the terrace, and shouting that the police were responsible for the death of one of their comrades.

The Government, fearing further trouble and wishing to avoid any disturbance on the day of the funeral of the victim of the riot in the Place Sorbonne, deceived the public as to the hour when it would occur. This exasperated the students so that they began one of those demonstrations for which Paris is famous. By 3 P.M. the next day the Quartier Latin was in a state of siege—these poets and painters and sculptors and musicians tore up the rue Jacob and constructed barricades near the hospital where their comrade had died. They tore up the rue Bonaparte, too, at the Place St. Germain des Prés, and built barricades, composed of overturned omnibuses and tramcars and newspaper booths. They smashed windows and everything else in sight, to get even with the Government and the smiling deputies and the murderous police—and then the troops came, and the affair took a different turn. In three days thirty thousand troops were in Paris—principally cavalry, many of the regiments coming from as far away as the center of France.

ÉCOLE DES BEAUX ARTS

With these and the police and the Garde Républicaine against them, the students melted away like a handful of snow in the sun; but the demonstrations continued spasmodically for two or three days longer, and the little crooked streets, like the rue du Four, were kept clear by the cavalry trotting abreast—in and out and dodging around corners—their black horse-tail plumes waving and helmets shining. It is sufficient to say that the vast army of artists and poets were routed to a man and driven back into the more peaceful atmosphere of their studios.

But the "Bullier" is closing and the crowd is pouring out into the cool air. I catch a glimpse of Yvonne with six students all in one fiacre, but Yvonne has been given the most comfortable place. They have put her in the hood, and the next instant they are rattling away to the Panthéon for supper.

If you walk down with the rest, you will pass dozens of jolly groups singing and romping and dancing along down the "Boul' Miche" to the taverne, for a bock and some écrivisse. With youth, good humor, and a "louis," all the world seems gay!

CHAPTER IV

❧

BAL DES QUAT'Z' ARTS

❧

f all the balls in Paris, the annual "Bal des Quat'z' Arts" stands unique. This costume ball is given every year, in the spring, by the students of the different ateliers, each atelier vying with the others in creation of the various floats and cortéges, and in the artistic effect and historical correctness of the costumes.

The first "Quat'z' Arts" ball was given in 1892. It was a primitive affair, compared with the later ones, but it was a success, and immediately the "Quat'z' Arts" Ball was put into the hands of clever organizers, and became a studied event in all its artistic sense. Months are spent in the creation of spectacles and in the costuming of students and models. Prizes are given for the most successful organizations, and a jury composed of painters and sculptors passes upon your costume as you enter the ball, and if you do not come up to their artistic standard you are unceremoniously turned away. Students who have been successful in getting into the "Quat'z' Arts" for years often fail to pass into this bewildering display of beauty and brains, owing to their costume not possessing enough artistic originality or merit to pass the jury.

It is, of course, a difficult matter for one who is not an enrolled member of one of the great ateliers of painting, architecture, or sculpture to get into the "Quat'z' Arts," and even after one's ticket is assured, you may fail to pass the jury.

Imagine this ball, with its procession of moving tableaux. A huge float comes along, depicting the stone age and the primitive man, every detail carefully studied from the museums. Another represents the last day of Babylon. One sees a nude captive, her golden hair and white flesh in contrast with the black velvet litter on which she is bound, being carried by a dozen stalwart blackamoors, followed by camels bearing nude slaves and the spoils of a captured city.

As the ball continues until daylight, it resembles a bacchanalian fête in the days of the Romans. But all through it, one is impressed by its artistic completeness, its studied splendor, and permissible license, so long as a costume (or the lack of it) produces an artistic result. One sees the mise en scène of a barbaric court produced by the architects of an atelier, all the various details constructed from carefully studied sketches, with maybe a triumphal throne of some barbaric king, with his slaves, the whole costumed and done in a studied magnificence that takes one's breath away. Again an atelier of painters may reproduce the frieze of the Parthenon in color; another a float or a decoration, suggesting the works of their master.

The room becomes a thing of splendor, for it is as gorgeous a spectacle as the cleverest of the painters, sculptors, and architects can make it, and is the result of careful study—and all for the love of it!—for the great "Quat'z' Arts" ball is an event looked forward to for months. Special instructions are issued to the different ateliers while the ball is in preparation, and the following one is a translation in part from the notice issued before the great ball of '99. As this is a special and private notice to the atelier, its contents may be interesting:

BAL DES QUAT'Z' ARTS,
Moulin Rouge, 21 April, 1899.

Doors open at 10 P.M. and closed at midnight.

The card of admission is absolutely personal, to be taken by the committee before the opening of the ball.

The committee will be masked, and comrades without their personal card will be refused at the door. The cards must carry the name and quality of the artist, and bear the stamp of his atelier.

Costumes are absolutely necessary. The soldier—the dress suit, black or in color—the monk—the blouse—the domino—kitchen boy—loafer—bicyclist, and other nauseous types, are absolutely prohibited.

Should the weather be bad, comrades are asked to wait in their carriages, as the committee in control cannot, under any pretext, neglect guarding the artistic effect of the ball during any confusion that might ensue.

A great "feed" will take place in the grand hall; the buffet will serve as usual individual suppers and baskets for two persons.

The committee wish especially to bring the attention of their comrades to the question of women, whose cards of admission must be delivered as soon as possible, so as to enlarge their attendance—always insufficient.

Prizes (champagne) will be distributed to the ateliers who may distinguish themselves by the artistic merit and beauty of their female display.

All the women who compete for these prizes will be assembled on the grand staircase before the orchestra. The nude, as always, is PROHIBITED!?!

The question of music at the head of the procession is of the greatest importance, and those comrades who are musical will please give their names to the delegates of the ateliers. Your good-will in this line is asked for—any great worthless capacity in this line will do, as they always play the same tune, "Les Pompiers!"

THE COMMITTEE—1899.

For days before the "Quat'z' Arts" ball, all is excitement among the students, who do as little work as possible and rest themselves for the great event. The favorite wit of the different ateliers is given the task of painting the banner of the atelier, which is carried at the head of the several cortéges. One of these, in Bouguereau's atelier, depicted their master caricatured as a cupid.

The boys once constructed an elephant with oriental trappings—an elephant that could wag his ears and lift his trunk and snort—and after the two fellows who formed respectfully the front and hind legs of this knowing beast had practised sufficiently to proceed with him safely, at the head of a cortége of slave girls, nautch dancers, and manacled captives, the big beast created a success in the procession at the "Quat'z' Arts" ball.

After the ball, in the gray morning light, they marched it back to the atelier, where it remained for some weeks, finally becoming such a nuisance, kicking around the atelier and getting in everybody's way, that the boys agreed to give it to the first junk-man that came around. But as no junk-man came, and as no one could be found to care for its now sadly battered hulk, its good riddance became a problem. What to do with the elephant! that was the question.

At last the two, who had sweltered in its dusty frame that eventful night of the "Quat'z' Arts," hit upon an idea. They marched it one day up the Boulevard St. Germain to the Café des deux Magots, followed by a crowd of people, who, when it reached the café, assembled around it, every one asking what it was for—or rather what it was?—for the beast had by now lost much of the resemblance of its former self. When half the street became blocked with the crowd, the two wise gentlemen crawled out of its fore and aft, and quickly mingled, unnoticed, with the bystanders. Then they disappeared in the crowd, leaving the elephant standing in the middle of the street. Those who had been expecting something to happen—a circus or the rest of the parade to come along—stood around for a while, and then the police, realizing that they had an elephant on their hands, carted the thing away, swearing meanwhile at the atelier and everyone connected with it.

The cafés near the Odéon, just before the beginning of the ball, are filled with students in costume; gladiators hobnob at the tables with savages in scanty attire—Roman soldiers and students, in the garb of the ancients, strut about or chat in groups, while the uninvited grisettes and models, who have not received invitations from the committee, implore them for tickets.

Tickets are not transferable, and should one present himself at the entrance of the ball with another fellow's ticket, he would run small chance of entering.

"What atelier?" commands the jury "Cormon."

The student answers, while the jury glance at his makeup.

"To the left!" cries the jury, and you pass in to the ball.

But if you are unknown they will say simply, "Connais-pas! To the right!" and you pass down a long covered alley—confident, if you are a "nouveau," that it leads into the ball-room—until you suddenly find yourself in the street, where your ticket is torn up and all hope of entering is gone.

It is hopeless to attempt to describe the hours until morning of this annual artistic orgy. As the morning light comes in through the windows, it is strange to see the effect of diffused daylight, electricity, and gas—the bluish light of early morning reflected on the flesh tones—upon nearly three thousand girls and students in costumes one might expect to see in a bacchanalian feast, just before the fall of Rome. Now they form a huge circle, the front row sitting on the floor, the second row squatting, the third seated in chairs, the fourth standing, so that all can see the dancing that begins in the morning hours—the wild impromptu dancing of the moment. A famous beauty, her black hair bound in a golden fillet with a circle wrought in silver and studded with Oriental turquoises clasping her superb torso, throws her sandals to the crowd and begins an Oriental dance—a thing of grace and beauty—fired with the intensity of the innate nature of this beautifully modeled daughter of Bohemia.

As the dance ends, there is a cry of delight from the great circle of barbarians. "Long live the Quat'z' Arts!" they cry, amid cheers for the dancer.

The ball closes about seven in the morning, when the long procession forms to return to the Latin Quarter, some marching, other students and girls in cabs and on top of them, many of the girls riding the horses. Down they come from the "Moulin Rouge," shouting, singing, and yelling. Heads are thrust out of windows, and a volley of badinage passes between the fantastic procession and those who have heard them coming.

Finally the great open court of the Louvre is reached—here a halt is made and a general romp occurs. A girl and a type climb one of the tall lamp-posts and prepare to do a mid-air balancing act, when rescued by the others. At last, at the end of all this horse-play, the march is resumed over the Pont du Carrousel and so on, cheered now by those going to work, until the Odéon is reached. Here the odd procession disbands; some go to their favorite cafés where the festivities are continued—some to sleep in their costumes or what remains of them, wherever fortune lands them—others to studios, where the gaiety is often kept up for days.

Ah! but life is not all "couleur de rose" in this true Bohemia.

"One day," says little Marguerite (she who lives in the rue Monge), "one eats and the next day one doesn't. It is always like that, is it not, monsieur?—and it costs so much to live, and so you see, monsieur, life is always a fight."

And Marguerite's brown eyes swim a little and her pretty mouth closes firmly.

"But where is Paul?" I ask.

"I do not know, monsieur," she replies quietly; "I have not seen him in ten days—the atelier is closed—I have been there every day, expecting to find him—he left no word with his concierge. I have been to his café too, but no one has seen him—you see, monsieur, Paul does not love me!"

I recall an incident that I chanced to see in passing the little shop where Marguerite works, that only confirms the truth of her realization. Paul had taken Marguerite back to the little shop, after their déjeuner together, and, as I passed, he stopped at the door with her, kissed her on both cheeks, and left her; but before they had gone a dozen paces, they ran back to embrace again. This occurred four times, until Paul and Marguerite finally parted. And, as he watched her little heels disappear up the wooden stairs to her work-room above, Paul blew a kiss to the pretty milliner at the window next door, and, taking a long whiff of his cigarette, sauntered off in the direction of his atelier whistling.

A MORNING'S WORK

It is ideal, this student life with its student loves of four years, but is it right to many an honest little comrade, who seldom knows an hour when she is away from her ami? who has suffered and starved and slaved with him through years of days of good and bad luck—who has encouraged him in his work, nursed him when ill, and made a thousand golden hours in this poet's or painter's life so completely happy, that he looks back on them in later life as never-to-be-forgotten? He remembers the good dinners at the little restaurant near his studio, where they dined among the old crowd. There were Lavaud the sculptor and Francine, with the figure of a goddess; Moreau, who played the cello at the opera; little Louise Dumont, who posed at Julian's, and old Jacquemart, the very soul of good fellowship, who would set them roaring with his inimitable humor.

What good dinners they were!—and how long they sat over their coffee and cigarettes under the trees in front of this little restaurant—often ten and twelve at a time, until more tables had to be pushed together for others of their good friends, who in passing would be hailed to join them. And how Marguerite used to sing all through dinner and how they would all sing, until it grew so late and so dark that they had to puff their cigarettes aglow over their plates, and yell to Madame Giraud for a light! And how the old lady would bustle out with the little oil lamp, placing it in the center of the long table amid the forest of vin ordinaires, with a "Voilà, mes enfants!" and a cheery word for all these good boys and girls, whom she regarded quite as her own children.

It seemed to them then that there would never be anything else but dinners at Madame Giraud's for as many years as they pleased, for no one ever thought of living out one's days, except in this good Bohemia of Paris. They could not imagine that old Jacquemart would ever die, or that La Belle Louise would grow old, and go back to Marseilles, to live with her dried-up old aunt, who sold garlic and bad cheese in a little box of a shop, up a crooked street! Or that Francine would marry Martin, the painter, and that the two would bury themselves in an adorable little spot in Brittany, where they now live in a thatched farm-house, full of Martin's pictures, and have a vegetable garden of their own—and a cow—and some children! But they DID!

A STUDIO DÉJEUNER

And those memorable dinners in the old studio back of the Gare Montparnasse! when paints and easels were pushed aside, and the table spread, and the piano rolled up beside it. There was the buying of the chicken, and the salad that Francine would smother in a dressing into which she would put a dozen different things—herbs and spices and tiny white onions! And what a jolly crowd came to these impromptu feasts! How much noise they used to make! How they danced and sang until the gray morning light would creep in through the big skylight, when all these good bohemians would tiptoe down the waxed stairs, and slip past the different ateliers for fear of waking those painters who might be asleep—a thought that never occurred to them until broad daylight, and the door had been opened, after hours of pandemonium and music and noise!

In a little hotel near the Odéon, there lived a family of just such bohemians—six struggling poets, each with an imagination and a love of good wine and good dinners and good times that left them continually in a state of bankruptcy! As they really never had any money—none that ever lasted for more than two days and two nights at the utmost, their good landlord seldom saw a sou in return for his hospitable roof, which had sheltered these six great minds who wrote of the moon, and of fate, and fortune, and love.

For days they would dream and starve and write. Then followed an auction sale of the total collection of verses, hawked about anywhere and everywhere among the editeurs, like a crop of patiently grown fruit. Having sold it, literally by the yard, they would all saunter up the "Boul' Miche," and forget their past misery, in feasting, to their hearts' content, on the good things of life. On days like these, you would see them passing, their black-brimmed hats adjusted jauntily over their poetic locks—their eyes beaming with that exquisite sense of feeling suddenly rich, that those who live for art's sake know! The keenest of pleasures lie in sudden contrasts, and to these six poetic, impractical Bohemians, thus suddenly raised from the slough of despond to a state where they no longer trod with mortals—their cup of happiness was full and spilling over. They must not only have a good time, but so must everyone around them. With their great riches, they would make the world gay as long as it lasted, for when it was over they knew how sad life would be. For a while—then they would scratch away—and have another auction!

DAYLIGHT

Unlike another good fellow, a painter whom I once knew, who periodically found himself without a sou, and who would take himself, in despair, to his lodgings, make his will, leaving most of his immortal works to his English aunt, go to bed, and calmly await death! In a fortunate space of time his friends, who had been hunting for him all over the Quarter, would find him at last and rescue him from his chosen tomb; or his good aunt, fearing he was ill, would send a draft! Then life would, to this impractical philosopher, again become worth living. He would dispatch a "petit bleu" to Marcelle; and the two would meet at the Café Cluny, and dine at La Perruse on filet de sole au vin blanc, and a bottle of Haut Barsac—the bottle all cobwebs and cradled in its basket—the garçon, as he poured its golden contents, holding his breath meanwhile lest he disturb its long slumber.

There are wines that stir the soul, and this was one of them—clear as a topaz and warming as the noonday sun—the same warmth that had given it birth on its hillside in Bordeaux, as far back as '82. It warmed the heart of Marcelle, too, and made her cheeks glow and her eyes sparkle—and added a rosier color to her lips. It made her talk—clearly and frankly, with a full and a happy heart, so that she confessed her love for this "bon garçon" of a painter, and her supreme admiration for his work and the financial success he had made with his art. All of which this genial son of Bohemia drank in with a feeling of pride, and he would swell out his chest and curl the ends of his long mustache upwards, and sigh like a man burdened with money, and secure in his ability and success, and with a peaceful outlook into the future—and the fact that Marcelle loved him of all men! They would linger long over their coffee and cigarettes, and then the two would stroll out under the stars and along the quai, and watch the little Seine boats crossing and recrossing, like fireflies, and the lights along the Pont Neuf reflected deep down like parti-colored ribbons in the black water.

CHAPTER V

※

"A DÉJEUNER AT LAVENUE'S"

※

If you should chance to breakfast at "Lavenue's," or, as it is called, the "Hôtel de France et Bretagne," for years famous as a rendezvous of men celebrated in art and letters, you will be impressed first with the simplicity of the three little rooms forming the popular side of this restaurant, and secondly with the distinguished appearance of its clientèle.

MADEMOISELLE FANNY AND HER STAFF

As you enter the front room, you pass good Mademoiselle Fanny at the desk, a cheery, white-capped, genial old lady, who has sat behind that desk for forty years, and has seen many a "bon garçon" struggle up the ladder of fame—from the days when he was a student at the Beaux-Arts, until his name became known the world over. It has long been a favorite restaurant with men like Rodin, the sculptor—and Colin, the painter—and the late Falguière—and Jean Paul Laurens and Bonnat, and dozens of others equally celebrated—and with our own men, like Whistler and Sargent and Harrison, and St. Gaudens and Macmonnies.

These three plain little rooms are totally different from the "other side," as it is called, of the Maison Lavenue. Here one finds quite a gorgeous café, with a pretty garden in the rear, and another room—opening into the garden—done in delicate green lattice and mirrors. This side is far more expensive to dine in than the side with the three plain little rooms, and the gentlemen with little red ribbons in their buttonholes; but as the same good cook dispenses from the single big kitchen, which serves for the dear and the cheap side the same good things to eat at just half the price, the reason for the popularity of the "cheap side" among the crowd who come here daily is evident.

RODIN

It is a quiet, restful place, this Maison Lavenue, and the best place I know in which to dine or breakfast from day to day. There is an air of intime and cosiness about Lavenue's that makes one always wish to return.

You will see a family of rich bourgeois enter, just in from the country, for the Montparnasse station is opposite. The fat, sunburned mama, and the equally rotund and genial farmer-papa, and the pretty daughter, and the newly married son and his demure wife, and the two younger children—and all talking and laughing over a good dinner with champagne, and many toasts to the young couple—and to mama and papa, and little Josephine—with ices, and fruit, and coffee, and liqueur to follow.

All these you will see at Lavenue's on the "cheap side"—and the beautiful model, too, who poses for Courbel, who is breakfasting with one of the jeunesse of Paris. The waiters after 2 P.M. dine in the front room with the rest, and jump up now and then to wait on madame and monsieur.

It is a very democratic little place, this popular side of the house of M. Lavenue, founded in 1854.

And there is a jolly old painter who dines there, who is also an excellent musician, with an ear for rhythm so sensitive that he could never go to sleep unless the clock in his studio ticked in regular time, and at last was obliged to give up his favorite atelier, with its picturesque garden——

"For two reasons, monsieur," he explained to me excitedly; "a little girl on the floor below me played a polka—the same polka half the day—always forgetting to put in the top note; and the fellow over me whistled it the rest of the day and put in the top note false; and so I moved to the rue St. Pères, where one only hears, within the cool court-yard, the distant hum of the busy city. The roar of Paris, so full of chords and melody! Listen to it sometimes, monsieur, and you will hear a symphony!"

"LA FILLE DE LA BLANCHISSEUSE"
By Bellanger.—Estampe Moderne

And Mademoiselle Fanny will tell you of the famous men she has known for years, and how she has found the most celebrated of them simple in their tastes, and free from ostentation—"in fact it is always so, is it not, with les hommes célèbres? C'est toujours comme ça, monsieur, toujours!" and mentions one who has grown gray in the service of art and can count his decorations from half a dozen governments. Madame will wax enthusiastic—her face wreathed in smiles. "Ah! he is a bon garçon; he always eats with the rest, for three or four francs, never more! He is so amiable, and, you know, he is very celebrated and very rich"; and madame will not only tell you his entire history, but about his work—the beauty of his wife and how "aimables" his children are. Mademoiselle Fanny knows them all.

But the men who come here to lunch are not idlers; they come in, many of them, fresh from a hard morning's work in the studio. The tall sculptor opposite you has been at work, since his morning coffee, on a group for the government; another, bare-armed and in his flannel shirt, has been building up masses of clay, punching and modeling, and scraping away, all the morning, until he produces, in the rough, the body of a giantess, a huge caryatide that is destined, for the rest of her existence, to hold upon her broad shoulders part of the façade of an American building. The "giantess" in the flesh is lunching with him—a Juno-like woman of perhaps twenty-five, with a superb head well poised, her figure firm and erect. You will find her exceedingly interesting, quiet, and refined, and with a knowledge of things in general that will surprise you, until you discover she has, in her life as a model, been thrown daily in conversation with men of genius, and has acquired a smattering of the knowledge of many things—of art and literature—of the theater and its playwrights—plunging now and then into medicine and law and poetry—all these things she has picked up in the studios, in the cafés, in the course of her Bohemian life. This "vernis," as the French call it, one finds constantly among the women here, for their days are passed among men of intelligence and ability, whose lives and energy are surrounded and encouraged by an atmosphere of art.

In an hour, the sculptor and his Juno-like model will stroll back to the studio, where work will be resumed as long as the light lasts.

A TRUE TYPE

The painter breakfasting at the next table is hard at work on a decorative panel for a ceiling. It is already laid out and squared up, from careful pencil drawings. Two young architects are working for him, laying out the architectural balustrade, through which one, a month later, looks up at the allegorical figures painted against the dome of the blue heavens, as a background. And so the painter swallows his eggs, mayonnaise, and demi of beer, at a gulp, for he has a model coming at two, and he must finish this ceiling on time, and ship it, by a fast liner, to a millionaire, who has built a vault-like structure on the Hudson, with iron dogs on the lawn. Here this beautiful panel will be unrolled and installed in the dome of the hard-wood billiard-room, where its rich, mellow scheme of color will count as naught; and the cupids and the flesh-tones of the chic little model, who came at two, will appear jaundiced; and Aunt Maria and Uncle John, and the twins from Ithaca, will come in after the family Sunday dinner of roast beef and potatoes and rice pudding and ice-water, and look up into the dome and agree "it's grand." But the painter does not care, for he has locked up his studio, and taken his twenty thousand francs and the model—who came at two—with him to Trouville.

At night you will find a typical crowd of Bohemians at the Closerie des Lilas, where they sit under a little clump of trees on the sloping dirt terrace in front. Here you will see the true type of the Quarter. It is the farthest up the Boulevard St. Michel of any of the cafés, and just opposite the "Bal Bullier," on the Place de l'Observatoire. The terrace is crowded with its habitués, for it is out of the way of the stream of people along the "Boul' Miche." The terrace is quite dark, its only light coming from the café, back of a green hedge, and it is cool there, too, in summer, with the fresh night air coming from the Luxembourg Gardens. Below it is the café and restaurant de la Rotonde, a very well-built looking place, with its rounding façade on the corner.

At the entrance of every studio court and apartment, there lives the concierge in a box of a room generally, containing a huge feather-bed and furnished with a variety of things left by departing tenants to this faithful guardian of the gate. Many of these small rooms resemble the den of an antiquary with their odds and ends from the studios—old swords, plaster casts, sketches and discarded furniture—until the place is quite full. Yet it is kept neat and clean by madame, who sews all day and talks to her cat and to everyone who passes into the court-yard. Here your letters are kept, too, in one of a row of boxes, with the number of your atelier marked thereon.

At night, after ten, your concierge opens the heavy iron gate of your court by pulling a cord within reach of the family bed. He or she is waked up at intervals through the night to let into and out of a court full of studios those to whom the night is ever young. Or perhaps your concierge will be like old Père Valois, who has three pretty daughters who do the housework of the studios, as well as assist in the guardianship of the gate. They are very busy, these three daughters of Père Valois—all the morning you will see these little "femmes de ménage" as busy as bees; the artists and poets must be waked up, and beds made and studios cleaned. There are many that are never cleaned at all, but then there are many, too, who are not so fortunate as to be taken care of by the three daughters of Père Valois.

VOILÀ LA BELLE ROSE, MADAME!

There is no gossip within the quarter that your "femme de ménage" does not know, and over your morning coffee, which she brings you, she will regale you with the latest news about most of your best friends, including your favorite model, and madame from whom you buy your wine, always concluding with: "That is what I heard, monsieur,—I think it is quite true, because the little Marie, who is the femme de ménage of Monsieur Valentin, got it from Céleste Dauphine yesterday in the café in the rue du Cherche Midi."

In the morning, this demure maid-of-all-work will be in her calico dress with her sleeves rolled up over her strong white arms, but in the evening you may see her in a chic little dress, at the "Bal Bullier," or dining at the Panthéon, with the fellow whose studio is opposite yours.

A BUSY MORNING

Alice Lemaître, however, was a far different type of femme de ménage than any of the gossiping daughters of old Père Valois, and her lot was harder, for one night she left her home in one of the provincial towns, when barely sixteen, and found herself in Paris with three francs to her name and not a friend in this big pleasure-loving city to turn to. After many days of privation, she became bonne to a woman known as Yvette de Marcie, a lady with a bad temper and many jewels, to whom little Alice, with her rosy cheeks and bright eyes and willing disposition to work in order to live, became a person upon whom this fashionable virago of a demi-mondaine vented the worst that was in her—and there was much of this—until Alice went out into the world again. She next found employment at a baker's, where she was obliged to get up at four in the morning, winter and summer, and deliver the long loaves of bread at the different houses; but the work was too hard and she left. The baker paid her a trifle a week for her labor, while the attractive Yvette de Marcie turned her into the street without her wages. It was while delivering bread one morning to an atelier in the rue des Dames, that she chanced to meet a young painter who was looking for a good femme de ménage to relieve his artistic mind from the worries of housekeeping. Little Alice fairly cried when the good painter told her she might come at twenty francs a month, which was more money than this very grateful and brave little Brittany girl had ever known before.

"You see, monsieur, one must do one's best whatever one undertakes," said Alice to me; "I have tried every profession, and now I am a good femme de ménage, and I am 'bien contente.' No," she continued, "I shall never marry, for one's independence is worth more than anything else. When one marries," she said earnestly, her little brow in a frown, "one's life is lost; I am young and strong, and I have courage, and so I can work hard. One should be content when one is not cold and hungry, and I have been many times that, monsieur. Once I worked in a fabrique, where, all day, we painted the combs of china roosters a bright red for bon-bon boxes—hundreds and hundreds of them until I used to see them in my dreams; but the fabrique failed, for the patron ran away with the wife of a Russian. He was a very stupid man to have done that, monsieur, for he had a very nice wife of his own—a pretty brunette, with a charming figure; but you see, monsieur, in Paris it is always that way. C'est toujours comme ça."

CHAPTER VI

❧

"AT MARCEL LEGAY'S"

❧

J UST off the Boulevard St. Michel and up the narrow little rue Cujas, you will see at night the name "Marcel Legay" illumined in tiny gas-jets. This is a cabaret of chansonniers known as "Le Grillon," where a dozen celebrated singing satirists entertain an appreciative audience in the stuffy little hall serving as an auditorium. Here, nightly, as the pièce de résistance—and late on the programme (there is no printed one)—you will hear the Bard of Montmartre, Marcel Legay, raconteur, poet, musician, and singer; the author of many of the most popular songs of Montmartre, and a veteran singer in the cabarets.

MARCEL LEGAY

From these cabarets of the student quarters come many of the cleverest and most beautiful songs. Here men sing their own

68

creations, and they have absolute license to sing or say what they please; there is no mincing of words, and many times these rare bohemians do not take the trouble to hide their clever songs and satires under a double entente. No celebrated man or woman, known in art or letters, or connected with the Government— from the soldier to the good President of the République Française—is spared. The eccentricity of each celebrity is caught by them, and used in song or recitation.

Besides these personal caricatures, the latest political questions of the day—religion and the haut monde—come in for a large share of good-natured satire. To be cleverly caricatured is an honor, and should evince no ill-feeling, especially from these clever singing comedians, who are the best of fellows at heart; whose songs are clever but never vulgar; who sing because they love to sing; and whose versatility enables them to create the broadest of satires, and, again, a little song with words so pure, so human, and so pathetic, that the applause that follows from the silent room of listeners comes spontaneously from the heart.

It is not to be wondered at that "The Grillon" of Marcel Legay's is a popular haunt of the habitués of the Quarter, who crowd the dingy little room nightly. You enter the "Grillon" by way of the bar, and at the further end of the bar-room is a small anteroom, its walls hung in clever posters and original drawings. This anteroom serves as a sort of green-room for the singers and their friends; here they chat at the little tables between their songs— since there is no stage—and through this anteroom both audience and singers pass into the little hall. There is the informality of one of our own "smokers" about the whole affair.

Furthermore, no women sing in "Le Grillon"—a cabaret in this respect is different from a café concert, which resembles very much our smaller variety shows. A small upright piano, and in front of it a low platform, scarcely its length, complete the necessary stage paraphernalia of the cabaret, and the admission is generally a franc and a half, which includes your drink.

In the anteroom, four of the singers are smoking and chatting at the little tables. One of them is a tall, serious-looking fellow, in a black frock coat. He peers out through his black-rimmed eyeglasses with the solemnity of an owl—but you should hear his songs!—they treat of the lighter side of life, I assure you. Another singer has just finished his turn, and comes out of the smoky hall, wiping the perspiration from his short, fat neck. The audience is still applauding his last song, and he rushes back through the faded green velvet portières to bow his thanks.

A POET-SINGER

A broad-shouldered, jolly-looking fellow, in white duck trousers, is talking earnestly with the owl-like looking bard in eyeglasses. Suddenly his turn is called, and you follow him in, where, as soon as he is seen, he is welcomed by cheers from the students and girls, and an elaborate fanfare of chords on the piano. When this popular poet-singer has finished, there follows a round of applause and a pounding of canes, and then the ruddy-faced, gray-haired manager starts a three-times-three handclapping in unison to a pounding of chords on the piano. This is the proper ending to every demand for an encore in "Le Grillon," and it never fails to bring one.

It is nearly eleven when the curtain parts and Marcel Legay rushes hurriedly up the aisle and greets the audience, slamming his straw hat upon the lid of the piano. He passes his hand over his bald pate—gives an extra polish to his eyeglasses—beams with an irresistibly funny expression upon his audience— coughs—whistles—passes a few remarks, and then, adjusting his glasses on his stubby red nose, looks serio-comically over his roll of music. He is dressed in a long, black frock-coat reaching nearly to his heels. This coat, with its velvet collar, discloses a frilled white shirt and a white flowing bow scarf; these, with a pair of black-and-white check trousers, complete this every-day attire.

But the man inside these voluminous clothes is even still more eccentric. Short, indefinitely past fifty years of age, with a round face and merry eyes, and a bald head whose lower portion is framed in a fringe of long hair, reminding one of the coiffure of some pre-Raphaelite saint—indeed, so striking is this resemblance that the good bard is often caricatured with a halo surrounding this medieval fringe.

In the meantime, while this famous singer is selecting a song, he is overwhelmed with demands for his most popular ones. A dozen students and girls at one end of the little hall, now swimming in a haze of pipe and cigarette smoke, are hammering with sticks and parasols for "Le matador avec les pieds du vent"; another crowd is yelling for "La Goularde." Marcel Legay smiles at them all through his eyeglasses, then roars at them to keep quiet—and finally the clamor in the room gradually subsides— here and there a word—a giggle—and finally silence.

"Now, my children, I will sing to you the story of Clarette," says the bard; "it is a very sad histoire. I have read it," and he smiles and cocks one eye.

His baritone voice still possesses considerable fire, and in his heroic songs he is dramatic. In "The Miller who grinds for Love," the feeling and intensity and dramatic quality he puts into its rendition are stirring. As he finishes his last encore, amidst a round of applause, he grasps his hat from the piano, jams it over his bald pate with its celestial fringe, and rushes for the door. Here he stops, and, turning for a second, cheers back at the crowd, waving the straw hat above his head. The next moment he is having a cooling drink among his confrères in the anteroom.

Such "poet-singers" as Paul Delmet and Dominique Bonnaud have made the "Grillon" a success; and others like Numa Blés, Gabriel Montoya, D'Herval, Fargy, Tourtal, and Edmond Teulet—all of them well-known over in Montmartre, where they are welcomed with the same popularity that they meet with at "Le Grillon."

Genius, alas, is but poorly paid in this Bohemia! There are so many who can draw, so many who can sing, so many poets and writers and sculptors. To many of the cleverest, half a loaf is too often better than no bread.

You will find often in these cabarets and in the cafés and along the boulevard, a man who, for a few sous, will render a portrait or a caricature on the spot. You learn that this journeyman artist once was a well-known painter of the Quarter, who had drawn for years in the academies. The man at present is a wreck, as he sits in a café with portfolio on his knees, his black slouch hat drawn over his scraggly gray hair. But his hand, thin and drawn from too much stimulant and too little food, has lost none of its knowledge of form and line; the sketch is strong, true, and with a chic about it and a simplicity of expression that delight you. You ask why he has not done better.

"Ah!" he replies, "it is a long story, monsieur." So long and so much of it that he cannot remember it all! Perhaps it was the woman with the velvety black eyes—tall and straight—the best dancer in all Paris. Yes, he remembers some of it—long, miserable years—years of struggles and jealousy, and finally lies and fights and drunkenness; after it was all over, he was too gray and old and tired to care!

THE SATIRIST

One sees many such derelicts in Paris among these people who have worn themselves out with amusement, for here the world lives for pleasure, for "la grande vie!" To the man, every serious effort he is obliged to make trends toward one idea—that of the bon vivant—to gain success and fame, but to gain it with the idea of how much personal daily pleasure it will bring him. Ennui is a word one hears constantly; if it rains toute le monde est triste. To have one's gaiety interrupted is regarded as a calamity, and "tout le monde" will sympathize with you. To live a day without the pleasures of life in proportion to one's purse is considered a day lost.

If you speak of anything that has pleased you one will, with a gay rising inflection of the voice and a smile, say: "Ah! c'est gai là-bas—and monsieur was well amused while in that beautiful country?" "ah!—tiens! c'est gentil ça!" they will exclaim, as you enthusiastically continue to explain. They never dull your enthusiasm by short phlegmatic or pessimistic replies. And when you are sad they will condone so genuinely with you that you forget your disappointments in the charming pleasantry of their sympathy. But all this continual race for pleasure is destined in the course of time to end in ennui!

The Parisian goes into the latest sport because it affords him a new sensation. Being blasé of all else in life, he plunges into automobiling, buys a white and red racer—a ponderous flying juggernaut that growls and snorts and smells of the lower regions whenever it stands still, trembling in its anger and impatience to be off, while its owner, with some automobiling Marie, sits chatting on the café terrace over a cooling drink. The two are covered with dust and very thirsty; Marie wears a long dust-colored ulster, and he a wind-proof coat and high boots. Meanwhile, the locomotive-like affair at the curbstone is working itself into a boiling rage, until finally the brave chauffeur and his chic companion prepare to depart. Marie adjusts her white lace veil, with its goggles, and the chauffeur puts on his own mask as he climbs in; a roar—a snort, a cloud of blue gas, and they are gone!

There are other enthusiasts—those who go up in balloons!

"Ah, you should go ballooning!" one cries enthusiastically, "to be 'en ballon'—so poetic—so fin de siècle! It is a fantaisie charmante!"

In a balloon one forgets the world—one is no longer a part of it—no longer mortal. What romance there is in going up above everything with the woman one loves—comrades in danger— the ropes—the wicker cage—the ceiling of stars above one and Paris below no bigger than a gridiron! Paris! lost for the time from one's memory. How chic to shoot straight up among the drifting clouds and forget the sordid little world, even the memory of one's intrigues!

"Enfin seuls," they say to each other, as the big Frenchman and the chic Parisienne countess peer down over the edge of the basket, sipping a little chartreuse from the same traveling cup; she, with the black hair and white skin, and gowned "en ballon" in a costume by Paillard; he in his peajacket buttoned close under his heavy beard. They seem to brush through and against the clouds! A gentle breath from heaven makes the basket decline a little and the ropes creak against the hardwood clinch blocks. It grows colder, and he wraps her closer in his own coat.

"Courage, my child," he says; "see, we have gone a great distance; to-morrow before sundown we shall descend in Belgium."

"Horrible!" cries the Countess; "I do not like those Belgians."

"Ah! but you shall see, Thérèse, one shall go where one pleases soon; we are patient, we aeronauts; we shall bring credit to La Belle France; we have courage and perseverance; we shall give many dinners and weep over the failures of our brave comrades, to make the dirigible balloon 'pratique.' We shall succeed! Then Voilà! our déjeuner in Paris and our dinner where we will."

Thérèse taps her polished nails against the edge of the wicker cage and hums a little chansonette.

"Je t'aime"—she murmurs.

I did not see this myself, and I do not know the fair Thérèse or the gentleman who buttons his coat under his whiskers; but you should have heard one of these ballooning enthusiasts tell it to me in the Taverne du Panthéon the other night. His only regret seemed to be that he, too, could not have a dirigible balloon and a countess—on ten francs a week!

CHAPTER VII

"POCHARD"

Drunkards are not frequent sights in the Quarter; and yet when these people do get drunk, they become as irresponsible as maniacs. Excitable to a degree even when sober, these most wretched among the poor when drunk often appear in front of a café—gaunt, wild-eyed, haggard, and filthy—singing in boisterous tones or reciting to you with tense voices a jumble of meaningless thoughts.

The man with the matted hair, and toes out of his boots, will fold his arms melodramatically, and regard you for some moments as you sit in front of him on the terrace. Then he will vent upon you a torrent of abuse, ending in some jumble of socialistic ideas of his own concoction. When he has finished, he will fold his arms again and move on to the next table. He is crazy with absinthe, and no one pays any attention to him. On he strides up the "Boul' Miche," past the cafés, continuing his ravings. As long as he is moderately peaceful and confines his wandering brain to gesticulations and speech, he is let alone by the police.

You will see sometimes a man and a woman—a teamster out of work or with his wages for the day, and with him a creature—a blear-eyed, slatternly looking woman, in a filthy calico gown. The man clutches her arm, as they sing and stagger up past the cafés.

The woman holds in her claw-like hand a half-empty bottle of cheap red wine. Now and then they stop and share it; the man staggers on; the woman leers and dances and sings; a crowd forms about them. Some years ago this poor girl sat on Friday afternoons in the Luxembourg Gardens—her white parasol on her knees, her dainty, white kid-slippered feet resting on the little stool which the old lady, who rents the chairs, used to bring her. She was regarded as a bonne camarade in those days among the students—one of the idols of the Quarter! But she became impossible, and then an outcast! That women should become outcasts through the hopelessness of their position or the breaking down of their brains can be understood, but that men of ability should sink into the dregs and stay there seems incredible. But it is often so.

Near the rue Monge there is a small café and restaurant, a place celebrated for its onion soup and its chicken. From the tables outside, one can see into the small kitchen, with its polished copper sauce-pans hanging about the grill.

Lachaume, the painter, and I were chatting at one of its little tables, he over an absinthe and I over a coffee and cognac. I had dined early this fresh October evening, enjoying to the full the bracing coolness of the air, pungent with the odor of dry leaves and the faint smell of burning brush. The world was hurrying by—in twos and threes—hurrying to warm cafés, to friends, to lovers. The breeze at twilight set the dry leaves shivering. The sky was turquoise. The yellow glow from the shop windows— the blue-white sparkle of electricity like pendant diamonds— made the Quarter seem fuller of life than ever. These fall days make the little ouvrières trip along from their work with rosy cheeks, and put happiness and ambition into one's very soul.

A GROUP OF NEW STUDIOS

Soon the winter will come, with all the boys back from their country haunts, and Céleste and Mimi from Ostende. How gay it will be—this Quartier Latin then! How gay it always is in winter—and then the rainy season. Ah! but one cannot have everything. Thus it was that Lachaume and I sat talking, when suddenly a spectre passed—a spectre of a man, his face silent, white, and pinched—drawn like a mummy's.

A SCULPTOR'S MODEL

He stopped and supported his shrunken frame wearily on his crutches, and leaned against a neighboring wall. He made no sound—simply gazed vacantly, with the timidity of some animal, at the door of the small kitchen aglow with the light from the grill. He made no effort to approach the door; only leaned against the gray wall and peered at it patiently.

"A beggar," I said to Lachaume; "poor devil!"

"Ah! old Pochard—yes, poor devil, and once one of the handsomest men in Paris."

"What wrecked him?" I asked.

"What I'm drinking now, mon ami."

"Absinthe?"

"Yes—absinthe! He looks older than I do, does he not?" continued Lachaume, lighting a fresh cigarette, "and yet I'm twenty years his senior. You see, I sip mine—he drank his by the goblet," and my friend leaned forward and poured the contents of the carafe in a tiny trickling stream over the sugar lying in its perforated spoon.

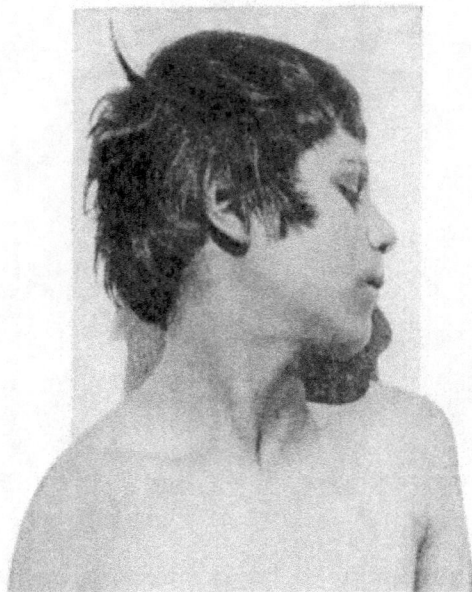

BOY MODEL

"Ah! those were great days when Pochard was the life of the Bullier," he went on; "I remember the night he won ten thousand francs from the Russian. It didn't last long; Camille Leroux had her share of it—nothing ever lasted long with Camille. He was once courrier to an Austrian Baron, I remember. The old fellow used to frequent the Quarter in summer, years ago—it was his hobby. Pochard was a great favorite in those days, and the Baron liked to go about in the Quarter with him, and of course Pochard was in his glory. He would persuade the old nobleman to prolong his vacation here. Once the Baron stayed through the winter and fell ill, and a little couturière in the rue de Rennes, whom the old fellow fell in love with, nursed him. He died the summer following, at Vienna, and left her quite a little property near Amiens. He was a good old Baron, a charitable old fellow among the needy, and a good bohemian besides; and he did much for Pochard, but he could not keep him sober!"

BOUGUEREAU AT WORK

"After the old man's death," my friend continued, "Pochard drifted from bad to worse, and finally out of the Quarter, somewhere into misery on the other side of the Seine. No one heard of him for a few years, until he was again recognized as being the same Pochard returned again to the Quarter. He was hobbling about on crutches just as you see him there. And now, do you know what he does? Get up from where you are sitting," said Lachaume, "and look into the back kitchen. Is he not standing there by the door—they are handing him a small bundle?"

"Yes," said I, "something wrapped in newspaper."

"Do you know what is in it?—the carcass of the chicken you have just finished, and which the garçon carried away. Pochard saw you eating it half an hour ago as he passed. It was for that he was waiting."

"To eat?" I asked.

"No, to sell," Lachaume replied, "together with the other bones he is able to collect—for soup in some poorest resort down by the river, where the boatmen and the gamins go. The few sous he gets will buy Pochard a big glass, a lump of sugar, and a spoon; into the goblet, in some equally dirty 'boîte,' they will pour him out his green treasure of absinthe. Then Pochard will forget the day—perhaps he will dream of the Austrian Baron—and try and forget Camille Leroux. Poor devil!"

GEROME

Marguerite Girardet, the model, also told me between poses in the studio the other day of just such a "pauvre homme" she once knew. "When he was young," she said, "he won a second prize at the Conservatoire, and afterward played first violin at the

Comique. Now he plays in front of the cafés, like the rest, and sometimes poses for the head of an old man!

A. MICHELENA

"Many grow old so young," she continued; "I knew a little model once with a beautiful figure, absolutely comme un bijou— pretty, too, and had she been a sensible girl, as I often told her, she could still have earned her ten francs a day posing; but she wanted to dine all the time with this and that one, and pose too, and in three months all her fine 'svelte' lines that made her a valuable model among the sculptors were gone. You see, I have posed all my life in the studios, and I am over thirty now, and you know I work hard, but I have kept my fine lines—because I go to bed early and eat and drink little. Then I have much to do at home; my husband and I for years have had a comfortable home; we take a great deal of pride in it, and it keeps me very busy to keep everything in order, for I pose very early some mornings and then go back and get déjeuner, and then back to pose again.

A SCULPTOR'S STUDIO

"In the summer," she went on, "we take a little place outside of Paris for a month, down the Seine, where my husband brings his work with him; he is a repairer of fans and objets d'art. You should come in and see us some time; it is quite near where you painted last summer. Ah yes," she exclaimed, as she drew her pink toes under her, "I love the country! Last year I posed nearly two months for Monsieur Z., the painter—en plein air; my skin was not as white as it is now, I can tell you—I was absolutely like an Indian!

FRÉMIET

"Once"—and Marguerite smiled at the memory of it—"I went to England to pose for a painter well known there. It was an important tableau, and I stayed there six months. It was a horrible place to me—I was always cold—the fog was so thick one could hardly see in winter mornings going to the studio. Besides, I could get nothing good to eat! He was a celebrated painter, a 'Sir,' and lived with his family in a big stone house with a garden. We had tea and cakes at five in the studio—always tea, tea, tea!—I can tell you I used to long for a good bottle of Madame Giraud's vin ordinaire, and a poulet. So I left and came back to Paris. Ah! quelle place! that Angleterre! J'étais toujours, toujours triste là! In Paris I make a good living; ten francs a day—that's not bad, is it? and my time is taken often a year ahead. I like to pose for the painters—the studios are cleaner than those of the sculptor's. Some of the sculptors' studios are so dirty—clay and dust over everything! Did you see Fabien's studio the other day when I posed for him? You thought it dirty? Tiens!—you should have seen it last year when he was working on the big group for the Exposition! It is clean now compared with what it was. You see, I go to my work in the plainest of clothes—a cheap print dress and everything of the simplest I can make, for in half an hour, left in those studios, they would be fit only for the blanchisseuse—the wax and dust are in and over everything! There is no time to change when one has not the time to go home at mid-day."

JEAN PAUL LAURENS

And so I learned much of the good sense and many of the economies in the life of this most celebrated model. You can see her superb figure wrought in marble and bronze by some of the most famous of modern French sculptors all over Paris.

There is another type of model you will see, too—one who rang my bell one sunny morning in response to a note written by my good friend, the sculptor, for whom this little Parisienne posed.

She came without her hat—this "vrai type"—about seventeen years of age—with exquisite features, her blue eyes shining under a wealth of delicate blonde hair arranged in the prettiest of fashions—a little white bow tied jauntily at her throat, and her exquisitely delicate, strong young figure clothed in a simple black dress. She had about her such a frank, childlike air! Yes, she posed for so and so, and so and so, but not many; she liked it better than being in a shop; and it was far more independent, for one could go about and see one's friends—and there were many of her girl friends living on the same street where this chic demoiselle lived.

At noon my drawing was finished. As she sat buttoning her boots, she looked up at me innocently, slipped her five francs for the morning's work in her reticule, and said:

"I live with mama, and mama never gives me any money to spend on myself. This is Sunday and a holiday, so I shall go with Henriette and her brother to Vincennes. It is delicious there under the trees."

It would have been quite impossible for me to have gone with them—I was not even invited; but this very serious and good little Parisienne, who posed for the figure with quite the same unconsciousness as she would have handed you your change over the counter of some stuffy little shop, went to Vincennes with Henriette and her brother, where they had a beautiful day—scrambling up the paths and listening to the band—all at the enormous expense of the artist; and this was how this good little Parisienne managed to save five francs in a single day!

OLD MAN MODEL

There are old-men models who knock at your studio too, and who are celebrated for their tangled gray locks, which they immediately uncover as you open your door. These unkempt-looking Father Times and Methuselahs prowl about the staircases of the different ateliers daily. So do little children—mostly Italians and all filthily dirty; swarthy, black-eyed, gypsy-looking girls and boys of from twelve to fifteen years of age, and Italian mothers holding small children—itinerant madonnas. These are the poorer class of models—the riff-raff of the Quarter—who get anywhere from a few sous to a few francs for a séance.

And there are four-footed models, too, for I know a kindly old horse who has served in many a studio and who has carried a score of the famous generals of the world and Jeanne d'Arcs to battle—in many a modern public square.

Chacun son métier!

CHAPTER VIII

THE LUXEMBOURG GARDENS

IN this busy Quarter, where so many people are confined throughout the day in work-shops and studios, a breathing-space becomes a necessity. The gardens of the Luxembourg, brilliant in flowers and laid out in the Renaissance, with shady groves and long avenues of chestnut-trees stretching up to the Place de l'Observatoire, afford the great breathing-ground for the Latin Quarter.

If one had but an hour to spend in the Quartier Latin, one could not find a more interesting and representative sight of student life than between the hours of four and five on Friday afternoon, when the military band plays in the Luxembourg Gardens. This is the afternoon when Bohemia is on parade. Then everyone flocks here to see one's friends—and a sort of weekly reception for the Quarter is held. The walks about the band-stand are thronged with students and girls, and hundreds of chairs are filled with an audience of the older people—shopkeepers and their families, old women in white lace caps, and gray-haired old men, many in straight-brimmed high hats of a mode of twenty years past. Here they sit and listen to the music under the cool shadow of the trees, whose rich foliage forms an arbor overhead—a roof of green leaves, through which the sunbeams stream and in which the fat, gray pigeons find a paradise.

THE CHILDREN'S SHOP—LUXEMBOURG GARDENS

There is a booth near-by where waffles, cooked on a small oven in the rear, are sold. In front are a dozen or more tables for ices and drinkables. Every table and chair is taken within hearing distance of the band. When these musicians of the army of France arrive, marching in twos from their barracks to the stand, it is always the signal for that genuine enthusiasm among the waiting crowd which one sees between the French and their soldiers.

If you chance to sit among the groups at the little tables, and watch the passing throng in front of you, you will see some queer "types," many of them seldom en evidence except on these Friday afternoons in the Luxembourg. Buried, no doubt, in some garret hermitage or studio, they emerge thus weekly to greet silently the passing world.

A tall poet stalks slowly by, reading intently, as he walks, a well-worn volume of verses—his faded straw hat shading the tip of his long nose. Following him, a boy of twenty, delicately featured, with that purity of expression one sees in the faces of the good—the result of a life, perhaps, given to his ideal in art. He wears his hair long and curling over his ears, with a long stray wisp over one eye, the whole cropped evenly at the back as it reaches his black velvet collar. He wears, too, a dove-gray vest of fine corduroy, buttoned behind like those of the clergy, and a velvet tam-o'-shanter-like cap, and carries between his teeth a small pipe with a long goose-quill stem. You can readily see that to this young man with high ideals there is only one corner of the world worth living in, and that lies between the Place de l'Observatoire and the Seine.

Three students pass, in wide broadcloth trousers, gathered in tight at the ankles, and wearing wide-brimmed black hats. Hanging on the arm of one of the trio is a short snub-nosed girl, whose Cleo-Merodic hair, flattened in a bandeau over her ears, not only completely conceals them, but all the rest of her face, except her two merry black eyes and her saucy and neatly rouged lips. She is in black bicycle bloomers and a white, short duck jacket—a straw hat with a wide blue ribbon band, and a fluffy piece of white tulle tied at the side of her neck.

The throng moves slowly by you. It is impossible, in such a close crowd, to be in a hurry; besides, one never is here.

Near-by sit two old ladies, evidently concierges from some atelier court. One holds the printed program of the music, cut carefully from her weekly newspaper; it is cheaper than buying one for two sous, and these old concierges are economical.

In this Friday gathering you will recognize dozens of faces which you have seen at the "Bal Bullier" and the cafés.

The girl in the blue tailor-made dress, with the little dog, who you remember dined the night before at the Panthéon, is walking now arm in arm with a tall man in black, a mourning band about his hat. The girl is dressed in black, too—a mark of respect to her ami by her side. The dog, who is so small that he slides along the walk every time his chain is pulled, is now tucked under her arm.

One of the tables near the waffle stand is taken by a group of six students and four girls. All of them have arrived at the table in the last fifteen minutes—some alone, some in twos. The girl in the scarlet gown and white kid slippers, who came with the queer-looking "type" with the pointed beard, is Yvonne Gallois—a bonne camarade. She keeps the rest in the best of spirits, for she is witty, this Yvonne, and a great favorite with the crowd she is with. She is pretty, too, and has a whole-souled good-humor about her that makes her ever welcome. The fellow she came with is Delmet the architect—a great wag—lazy, but full of fun—and genius.

The little girl sitting opposite Yvonne is Claire Dumont. She is explaining a very sad "histoire" to the "type" next to her, intense in the recital of her woes. Her alert, nervous little face is a study; when words and expression fail, she shrugs her delicate shoulders, accenting every sentence with her hands, until it seems as if her small, nervous frame could express no more— and all about her little dog "Loisette!"

AT THE HEAD OF THE LUXEMBOURG GARDENS

"Yes, the villain of a concierge at Edmond's studio swore at him twice, and Sunday, when Edmond and I were breakfasting late, the old beast saw 'Loisette' on the stairs and threw water over her; she is a sale bête, that grosse femme! She shall see what it will cost her, the old miser; and you know I have always been most amiable with her. She is jealous of me—that is it—oh! I am certain of it. Because I am young and happy. Jealous of me! that's funny, is it not? The old pig! Poor 'Loisette'—she shivered all night with fright and from being wet. Edmond and I are going to find another place. Yes, she shall see what it will be there without us—with no one to depend upon for her snuff and her wine. If she were concierge at Edmond's old atelier she would be treated like that horrid old Madame Fouquet."

The boys in the atelier over her window hated this old Madame Fouquet, I remember. She was always prying about and complaining, so they fished up her pet gold-fish out of the aquarium on her window-sill, and fried them on the atelier stove, and put them back in the window on a little plate all garnished with carrots. She swore vengeance and called in the police, but to no avail. One day they fished up the parrot in its cage, and the green bird that screamed and squawked continually met a speedy and painless death and went off to the taxidermist. Then the cage was lowered in its place with the door left ajar, and the old woman felt sure that her pet had escaped and would someday find his way back to her—a thing this garrulous bird would never have thought of doing had he had any say in the matter.

So the old lady left the door of the cage open for days in the event of his return, and strange to tell, one morning Madame Fouquet got up to quarrel with her next-door neighbor, and, to her amazement, there was her green pet on his perch in his cage. She called to him, but he did not answer; he simply stood on his wired legs and fixed his glassy eyes on her, and said not a word—while the gang of Indians in the windows above yelled themselves hoarse.

It was just such a crowd as this that initiated a "nouveau" once in one of the ateliers. They stripped the new-comer, and, as is often the custom on similar festive occasions, painted him all over with sketches, done in the powdered water-colors that come in glass jars. They are cheap and cover a lot of surface, so that the gentleman in question looked like a human picture-gallery. After the ceremony, he was put in a hamper and deposited, in the morning, in the middle of the Pont des Arts, where he was subsequently found by the police, who carted him off in a cab.

THE FONTAINE DE MEDICIS

But you must see more of this vast garden of the Luxembourg to appreciate truly its beauty and its charm. Filled with beautiful sculpture in bronze and marble, with its musée of famous modern pictures bought by the Government, with flower-beds brilliant in geraniums and fragrant in roses, with the big basin spouting a jet of water in its center, where the children sail their boats, and with that superb "Fontaine de Medicis" at the end of a long, rectangular basin of water—dark as some pool in a forest brook, the green vines trailing about its sides, shaded by the rich foliage of the trees overhead.

On the other side of the Luxembourg you will find a garden of roses, with a rich bronze group of Greek runners in the center, and near it, back of the long marble balustrade, a croquet ground—a favorite spot for several veteran enthusiasts who play here regularly, surrounded for hours by an interested crowd who applaud and cheer the participants in this passé sport.

This is another way of spending an afternoon at the sole cost of one's leisure. It takes but little to amuse these people!

Often at the Punch and Judy show near-by, you will see two old gentlemen,—who may have watched this same Punch and Judy show when they were youngsters,—and who have been sitting for half an hour, waiting for the curtain of the miniature theater to rise. It is popular—this small "Théâtre Guignol," and the benches in front are filled with the children of rich and poor, who scream with delight and kick their little, fat bare legs at the first shrill squeak of Mr. Punch. The three who compose the staff of this tiny attraction have been long in its service—the old harpist, and the good wife of the showman who knows every child in the neighborhood, and her husband who is Mr. Punch, the hangman, and the gendarme, and half a dozen other equally historical personages. A thin, sad-looking man, this husband, gray-haired, with a careworn look in his deep-sunken eyes, who works harder hourly, daily, yearly, to amuse the heart of a child than almost anyone I know.

The little box of a theater is stifling hot in summer, and yet he must laugh and scream and sing within it, while his good wife collects the sous, talking all the while to this and to that child whom she has known since its babyhood; chatting with the nurses decked out in their gay-colored, Alsatian bows, the ribbons reaching nearly to the ground.

A French nurse is a gorgeous spectacle of neatness and cleanliness, and many of the younger ones, fresh from country homes in Normandy and Brittany, with their rosy cheeks, are pictures of health. Wherever you see a nurse, you will see a "piou-piou" not far away, which is a very belittling word for the red-trousered infantryman of the République Française.

Surrounding the Palais du Luxembourg, these "piou-pious," less fortunate for the hour, stand guard in the small striped sentry-boxes, musket at side, or pace stolidly up and down the flagged walk. Marie, at the moment, is no doubt with the children of the rich Count, in a shady spot near the music. How cruel is the fate of many a gallant "piou-piou"!

Farther down the gravel-walk strolls a young Frenchman and his fiancée—the mother of his betrothed inevitably at her side! It is under this system of rigid chaperonage that the young girl of France is given in marriage. It is not to be wondered at that many of them marry to be free, and that many of the happier marriages have begun with an elopement!

THE PALACE OF THE LUXEMBOURG

The music is over, and the band is filing out, followed by the crowd. A few linger about the walks around the band-stand to chat. The old lady who rents the chairs is stacking them up about the tree-trunks, and long shadows across the walks tell of the approaching twilight. Overhead, among the leaves, the pigeons coo. For a few moments the sun bathes the great garden in a pinkish glow, then drops slowly, a blood-red disk, behind the trees. The air grows chilly; it is again the hour to dine—the hour when Paris wakes.

In the smaller restaurants of the Quarter one often sees some strange contrasts among these true bohemians, for the Latin Quarter draws its habitués from every part of the globe. They are not all French—these happy-go-lucky fellows, who live for the day and let the morrow slide. You will see many Japanese— some of them painters—many of them taking courses in political economy, or in law; many of them titled men of high rank in their own country, studying in the schools, and learning, too, with that thoroughness and rapidity which are ever characteristic of their race. You will find, too, Brazilians; gentlemen from Haiti of darker hue; Russians, Poles, and Spaniards—men and women from every clime and every station in life. They adapt themselves to the Quarter and become a part of this big family of Bohemia easily and naturally.

In this daily atmosphere only the girl-student from our own shores seems out of place. She will hunt for some small restaurant, sacred in its exclusiveness and known only to a dozen bon camarades of the Quarter. Perhaps this girl-student, it may be, from the West and her cousin from the East will discover some such cosy little boîte on their way back from their atelier. To two other equally adventurous female minds they will impart this newest find; after that you will see the four dining there nightly together, as safe, I assure you, within these walls of Bohemia as they would be at home rocking on their Aunt Mary's porch.

There is, of course, considerable awkwardness between these bon camarades, to whom the place really belongs, and these very innocent new-comers, who seek a table by themselves in a corner under the few trees in front of the small restaurant. And yet everyone is exceedingly polite to them. Madame the patronne hustles about to see that the dinner is warm and nicely served;

and Henriette, who is waiting on them, none the less attentive, although she is late for her own dinner, which she will sit down to presently with madame the patronne, the good cook, and the other girls who serve the small tables.

WHAT IS GOING ON AT THE THEATERS

This later feast will be augmented perhaps by half the good boys and girls who have been dining at the long table. Perhaps they will all come in and help shell the peas for tomorrow's dinner. And yet this is a public place, where the painters come, and where one pays only for what one orders. It is all very interesting to the four American girls, who are dining at the small table. "It is so thoroughly bohemian!" they exclaim.

But what must Mimi think of these silent and exclusive strangers, and what, too, must the tall girl in the bicycle bloomers think, and the little girl who has been ill and who at the moment is dining with Renould, the artist, and whom every one—even to the cook, is so glad to welcome back after her long illness? There is an unsurmountable barrier between the Americans at the little table in the corner and that jolly crowd of good and kindly people at the long one, for Mimi and Henriette and the little girl who has been so ill, and the French painters and sculptors with them, cannot understand either the language of these strangers or their views of life.

"Florence!" exclaims one of the strangers in a whisper, "do look at that queer little 'type' at the long table—the tall girl in black actually kissed him!"

"You don't mean it!"

"Yes, I do—just now. Why, my dear, I saw it plainly!"

Poor culprits! There is no law against kissing in the open air in Paris, and besides, the tall girl in black has known the little "type" for a Parisienne age—thirty days or less.

The four innocents, who have coughed through their soup and whispered through the rest of the dinner, have now finished and are leaving, but if those at the long table notice their departure, they do not show it. In the Quarter it is considered the height of rudeness to stare. You will find these Suzannes and Marcelles exceedingly well-bred in the little refinements of life, and you will note a certain innate dignity and kindliness in their bearing toward others, which often makes one wish to uncover his head in their presence.

CHAPTER IX

꒳

"THE RAGGED EDGE
OF THE
QUARTER"

꒳

THERE are many streets of the Quarter as quiet as those of a country village. Some of them, like the rue Vaugirard, lead out past gloomy slaughter-houses and stables, through desolate sections of vacant lots, littered with the ruins of factory and foundry whose tall, smoke-begrimed chimneys in the dark stand like giant sentries, as if pointing a warning finger to the approaching pedestrian, for these ragged edges of the Quarter often afford at night a lurking-ground for footpads.

In just such desolation there lived a dozen students, in a small nest of studios that I need not say were rented to them at a price within their ever-scanty means. It was marveled at among the boys in the Quarter that any of these exiles lived to see the light of another day, after wandering back at all hours of the night to their stronghold.

Possibly their sole possessions consisted of the clothes they had on, a few bad pictures, and their several immortal geniuses. That the gentlemen with the sand-bags knew of this I am convinced, for the students were never molested. Verily, Providence lends a strong and ready arm to the drunken man and the fool!

The farther out one goes on the rue Vaugirard, the more desolate and forbidding becomes this long highway, until it terminates at the fortifications, near which is a huge, open field, kept clear of such permanent buildings as might shelter an enemy in time of war. Scattered over this space are the hovels of squatters and gipsies—fortune-telling, horse-trading vagabonds, whose living-vans at certain times of the year form part of the smaller fairs within the Quarter.

And very small and unattractive little fairs they are, consisting of half a dozen or more wagons, serving as a yearly abode for these shiftless people; illumined at night by the glare of smoking oil torches. There is, moreover, a dingy tent with a half-drawn red curtain that hides the fortune-telling beauty; and a traveling shooting-gallery, so short that the muzzle of one's rifle nearly rests upon the painted lady with the sheet-iron breastbone, centered by a pinhead of a bull's-eye which never rings. There is often a small carousel, too, which is not only patronized by the children, but often by a crowd of students—boys and girls, who literally turn the merry-go-round into a circus, and who for the time are cheered to feats of bareback riding by the enthusiastic bystanders.

These little Quarter fêtes are far different from the great fête de Neuilly across the Seine, which begins at the Porte Maillot, and continues in a long, glittering avenue of side-shows, with mammoth carousels, bizarre in looking-glass panels and golden figures. Within the circle of all this throne-like gorgeousness, a horse-power organ shakes the very ground with its clarion blasts, while pink and white wooden pigs, their tails tied up in bows of colored ribbons, heave and swoop round and round, their backs loaded with screaming girls and shouting men.

It was near this very same Port Maillot, in a colossal theater, built originally for the representation of one of the Kiralfy ballets, that a fellow student and myself went over from the Quarter one night to "supe" in a spectacular and melodramatic pantomime, entitled "Afrique à Paris." We were invited by the sole proprietor and manager of the show—an old circus-man, and one of the shrewdest, most companionable, and intelligent of men, who had traveled the world over. He spoke no language but his own unadulterated American. This, with his dominant personality, served him wherever fortune carried him!

So, accepting his invitation to play alternately the dying soldier and the pursuing cannibal under the scorching rays of a tropical limelight, and with an old pair of trousers and a flannel shirt wrapped in a newspaper, we presented ourselves at the appointed hour, at the edge of the hostile country.

Here we found ourselves surrounded by a horde of savages who needed no greasepaint to stain their ebony bodies, and many of whose grinning countenances I had often recognized along our own Tenderloin. Besides, there were cowboys and "greasers" and diving elks, and a company of French Zouaves; the latter, in fact, seemed to be the only thing foreign about the show. Our friend, the manager, informed us that he had thrown the entire spectacle together in about ten days, and that he had gathered with ease, in two, a hundred of those dusky warriors, who had left their coat-room and barber-shop jobs in New York to find themselves stranded in Paris.

He was a hustler, this circus-man, and preceding the spectacle of the African war, he had entertained the audience with a short variety-show, to brace the spectacle. He insisted on bringing us around in front and giving us a box, so we could see for ourselves how good it really was.

During this forepart, and after some clever high trapeze work, the sensation of the evening was announced—a Signore, with an unpronounceable name, would train a den of ten forest-bred lions!

When the orchestra had finished playing "The Awakening of the Lion," the curtain rose, disclosing the nerveless Signore in purple tights and high-topped boots. A long, portable cage had been put together on the stage during the intermission, and within it the ten pacing beasts. There is something terrifying about the roar of a lion as it begins with its high-keyed moan, and descends in scale to a hoarse roar that seems to penetrate one's whole nervous system.

But the Signore did not seem to mind it; he placed one foot on the sill of the safety-door, tucked his short riding-whip under his arm, pulled the latch with one hand, forced one knee in the slightly opened door, and sprang into the cage. Click! went the iron door as it found its lock. Bang! went the Signore's revolver, as he drove the snarling, roaring lot into the corner of the cage. The smoke from his revolver drifted out through the bars; the house was silent. The trainer walked slowly up to the fiercest lion, who reared against the bars as he approached him, striking at the trainer with his heavy paws, while the others slunk into the opposite corner. The man's head was but half a foot now from the lion's; he menaced the beast with the little riding-whip; he almost, but did not quite strike him on the tip of his black nose that worked convulsively in rage. Then the lion dropped awkwardly, with a short growl, to his forelegs, and slunk, with the rest, into the corner. The Signore turned and bowed. It was the little riding-whip they feared, for they had never gauged its sting. Not the heavy iron bar within reach of his hand, whose force they knew. The vast audience breathed easier.

"An ugly lot," I said, turning to our friend the manager, who had taken his seat beside me.

"Yes," he mused, peering at the stage with his keen gray eyes; "green stock, but a swell act, eh? Wait for the grand finale. I've got a girl here who comes on and does art poses among the lions; she's a dream—French, too!"

A girl of perhaps twenty, enveloped in a bath gown, now appeared at the wings. The next instant the huge theater became dark, and she stood in full fleshings, in the center of the cage, brilliant in the rays of a powerful limelight, while the lions circled about her at the command of the trainer.

"Ain't she a peach?" said the manager, enthusiastically.

"Yes," said I, "she is. Has she been in the cages long?" I asked.

"No, she never worked with the cats before," he said; "she's new to the show business; she said her folks live in Nantes. She worked here in a chocolate factory until she saw my 'ad' last week and joined my show. We gave her a rehearsal Monday and we put her on the bill next night. She's a good looker with plenty of grit, and is a winner with the bunch in front."

"How did you get her to take the job?" I said.

"Well," he replied, "she balked at the act at first, but I showed her two violet notes from a couple of swell fairies who wanted the job, and after that she signed for six weeks."

"Who wrote the notes?" I said, queryingly.

"I wrote 'em!" he exclaimed dryly, and he bit the corner of his stubby mustache and smiled. "This is the last act in the olio, so you will have to excuse me. So long!" and he disappeared in the gloom.

There are streets and boulevards in the Quarter, sections of which are alive with the passing throng and the traffic of carts and omnibuses. Then one will come to a long stretch of massive buildings, public institutions, silent as convents—their interminable walls flanking garden or court.

The Boulevard St. Germain is just such a highway until it crosses the Boulevard St. Michel—the liveliest roadway of the Quarter. Then it seems to become suddenly inoculated with its bustle and life, and from there on is crowded with bourgeoise and animated with the commerce of market and shop.

An Englishman once was so fired with a desire to see the gay life of the Latin Quarter that he rented a suite of rooms on this same Boulevard St. Germain at about the middle of this long, quiet stretch. Here he stayed a fortnight, expecting daily to see from his "chambers" the gaiety of a Bohemia of which he had so often heard. At the end of his disappointing sojourn, he returned to London, firmly convinced that the gay life of the Latin Quarter was a myth. It was to him.

But the man from Denver, the "Steel King," and the two thinner gentlemen with the louis-lined waistcoats who accompanied him and whom Fortune had awakened in the far West one morning and had led them to "The Great Red Star copper mine"—a find which had ever since been a source of endless amusement to them—discovered the Quarter before they had been in Paris a day, and found it, too, "the best ever," as they expressed it.

They did not remain long in Paris, this rare crowd of seasoned genials, for it was their first trip abroad and they had to see Switzerland and Vienna, and the Rhine; but while they stayed they had a good time Every Minute.

The man from Denver and the Steel King sat at one of the small tables, leaning over the railing at the "Bal Bullier," gazing at the sea of dancers.

"Billy," said the man from Denver to the Steel King, "if they had this in Chicago they'd tear out the posts inside of fifteen minutes"—he wiped the perspiration from his broad forehead and pushed his twenty-dollar Panama on the back of his head.

"Ain't it a sight!" he mused, clinching the butt of his perfecto between his teeth. "Say!—say! it beats all I ever see," and he chuckled to himself, his round, genial face, with its double chin, wreathed in smiles.

"Say, George!" he called to one of the 'copper twins,' "did you get on to that little one in black that just went by—well! well!! well!!! In a minute!!"

Already the pile of saucers on their table reached a foot high—a record of refreshments for every Yvonne and Marcelle that had stopped in passing. Two girls approach.

"Certainly, sit right down," cried the Steel King. "Here, Jack,"—this to the aged garçon, "smoke up! and ask the ladies what they'll have"—all of which was unintelligible to the two little Parisiennes and the garçon, but quite clear in meaning to all three.

"Dis donc, garçon!" interrupted the taller of the two girls, "un café glacé pour moi."

"Et moi," answered her companion gayly, "Je prends une limonade!"

"Here! Hold on!" thundered good-humoredly the man from Denver; "git 'em a good drink. Rye, garsong! yes, that's it—whiskey—I see you're on, and two. Deux!" he explains, holding up two fat fingers, "all straight, friend—two whiskeys with seltzer on the side—see? Now go roll your hoop and git back with 'em."

"Oh, non, monsieur!" cried the two Parisiennes in one breath; "whiskey! jamais! ça pique et c'est trop fort."

At this juncture the flower woman arrived with a basketful of red roses.

"Voulez-vous des fleurs, messieurs et mesdames?" she asked politely.

"Certainly," cried the Steel King; "here, Maud and Mamie, take the lot," and he handed the two girls the entire contents of the basket. The taller buried her face for a moment in the red Jaqueminots and drank in their fragrance. When she looked up, two big tears trickled down to the corners of her pretty mouth. In a moment more she was smiling! The smaller girl gave a little cry of delight and shook her roses above her head as three other girls passed. Ten minutes later the two possessed but a single rose apiece—they had generously given all the rest away.

The "copper twins" had been oblivious of all this. They had been hanging over the low balustrade, engaged in a heart-to-heart talk with two pretty Quartier brunettes. It seemed to be really a case of love at first sight, carried on somewhat under difficulties, for the "copper twins" could not speak a word of French, and the English of the two chic brunettes was limited to "Oh, yes!" "Very well!" "Good morning," "Good evening," and

"I love you." The four held hands over the low railing, until the "copper twins" fairly steamed in talk; warmed by the sun of gaiety and wet by several rounds of Highland dew, they grew sad and earnest, and got up and stepped all over the Steel King and the man from Denver, and the two Parisiennes' daintily slippered feet, in squeezing out past the group of round tables back of the balustrade, and down on to the polished floor— where they are speedily lost to view in the maze of dancers, gliding into the whirl with the two brunettes. When the waltz is over they stroll out with them into the garden, and order wine, and talk of changing their steamer date.

The good American, with his spotless collar and his well-cut clothes, with his frankness and whole-souled generosity, is a study to the modern grisette. He seems strangely attractive to her, in contrast with a certain type of Frenchman, that is selfish, unfaithful, and mean—that jealousy makes uncompanionable and sometimes cruel. She will tell you that these pale, black-eyed, and black-bearded boulevardiers are all alike—lazy and selfish; so unlike many of the sterling, good fellows of the Quarter— Frenchmen of a different stamp, and there are many of these— rare, good Bohemians, with hearts and natures as big as all out-doors—"bons garçons," which is only another way of saying "gentlemen."

As you tramp along back to your quarters some rainy night you find many of the streets leading from the boulevards silent and badly lighted, except for some flickering lantern on the corner of a long block which sends the shadows scurrying across your path. You pass a student perhaps and a girl, hurrying home—a fiacre for a short distance is a luxury in the Quarter. Now you hear the click-clock of an approaching cab, the cocher half asleep on his box. The hood of the fiacre is up, sheltering the two inside from the rain. As the voiture rumbles by near a street-light, you catch a glimpse of a pink silk petticoat within and a pair of dainty, white kid shoes—and the glint of an officer's sword.

Farther on, you pass a silent gendarme muffled in his night cloak; a few doors farther on in a small café, a bourgeois couple, who have arrived on a late train no doubt to spend a month with relatives in Paris, are having a warming tipple before proceeding farther in the drizzling rain. They have, of course, invited the cocher to drink with them. They have brought all their pets and nearly all their household goods—two dogs, three bird-cages, their tiny occupants protected from the damp air by several folds of newspaper; a cat in a stout paper box with air holes, and two trunks, well tied with rope.

"Ah, yes, it has been a long journey!" sighs the wife. Her husband corroborates her, as they explain to the patronne of the café and to the cocher that they left their village at midday. Anything over two hours on the chemin-de-fer is considered a journey by these good French people!

As you continue on to your studio, you catch a glimpse of the lights of the Boulevard Montparnasse. Next a cab with a green light rattles by; then a ponderous two-wheeled cart lumbers along, piled high with red carrots as neatly arranged as cigars in a box—the driver asleep on his seat near his swinging lantern—and the big Normandy horses taking the way. It is late, for these carts are on their route to the early morning market—one of the great Halles. The tired waiters are putting up the shutters of the smaller cafés and stacking up the chairs. Now a cock crows lustily in some neighboring yard; the majority at least of the Latin Quarter has turned in for the night. A moment later you reach your gate, feel instinctively for your matches. In the darkness of the court a friendly cat rubs her head contentedly against your leg. It is the yellow one that sleeps in the furniture factory, and you pick her up and carry her to your studio, where, a moment later, she is crunching gratefully the remnant of the beau maquereau left from your déjeuner—for charity begins at home.

CHAPTER X

❧

EXILED

❧

cores of men, celebrated in art and in literature, have, for a longer or shorter period of their lives, been bohemians of the Latin Quarter. And yet these years spent in cafés and in studios have not turned them out into the world a devil-me-care lot of dreamers. They have all marched and sung along the "Boul' Miche"; danced at the "Bullier"; starved, struggled, and lived in the romance of its life. It has all been a part of their education, and a very important part too, in the development of their several geniuses, a development which in later life has placed them at the head of their professions. These years of camaraderie—of a life free from all conventionalities, in daily touch with everything about them, and untrammeled by public censure or the petty views of prudish or narrow minds, have left them free to cut a straight swath merrily toward the goal of their ideals, surrounded all the while by an atmosphere of art and good-fellowship that permeates the very air they breathe.

If a man can work at all, he can work here, for between the working-hours he finds a life so charming, that once having lived it he returns to it again and again, as to an old love.

How many are the romances of this student Quarter! How many hearts have been broken or made glad! How many brave spirits have suffered and worked on and suffered again, and at last won fame! How many have failed! We who come with a fresh eye know nothing of all that has passed within these quaint streets— only those who have lived in and through it know its full story.

THE MUSÉE CLUNY

Pochard has seen it; so has the little old woman who once danced at the opera; so have old Bibi La Purée, and Alphonse, the gray-haired garçon, and Mère Gaillard, the flower-woman. They have seen the gay boulevards and the cafés and generations of grisettes, from the true grisette of years gone by, in her dainty white cap and simple dress turned low at the throat, to the tailor-made grisette of to-day.

Yet the eyes of the little old woman still dance; they have not grown tired of this ever-changing kaleidoscope of human nature, this paradise of the free, where many would rather struggle on half starved than live a life of luxury elsewhere.

And the students are equally quixotic. I knew one once who lived in an air-castle of his own building—a tall, serious fellow, a sculptor, who always went tramping about in a robe resembling a monk's cowl, with his bare feet incased in coarse sandals; only his art redeemed these eccentricities, for he produced in steel and ivory the most exquisite statuettes. One at the Salon was the sensation of the day—a knight in full armor, scarcely half a foot in height, holding in his arms a nymph in flesh-tinted ivory, whose gentle face, upturned, gazed sweetly into the stern features behind the uplifted vizor; and all so exquisitely carved, so alive, so human, that one could almost feel the tender heart of this fair lady beating against the cold steel breastplate.

Another "bon garçon"—a painter whose enthusiasm for his art knew no bounds—craved to produce a masterpiece. This dreamer could be seen daily ferreting around the Quarter for a studio always bigger than the one he had. At last he found one that exactly fitted the requirements of his vivid imagination—a studio with a ceiling thirty feet high, with windows like the scenic ones next to the stage entrances of the theaters. Here at last he could give full play to his brush—no subject seemed too big for him to tackle; he would move in a canvas as big as a back flat to a third act, and commence on a "Fall of Babylon" or a "Carnage of Rome" with a nerve that was sublime! The choking dust of the arena—the insatiable fury of the tigers—the cowering of hundreds of unfortunate captives—and the cruel multitude above, seated in the vast circle of the hippodrome—all these did not daunt his zeal.

Once he persuaded a venerable old abbé to pose for his portrait. The old gentleman came patiently to his studio and posed for ten days, at the end of which time the abbé gazed at the result and said things which I dare not repeat—for our enthusiast had so far only painted his clothes; the face was still in its primary drawing.

"The face I shall do in time," the enthusiast assured the reverend man excitedly; "it is the effect of the rich color of your robe I wished to get. And may I ask your holiness to be patient a day longer while I put in your boots?"

"No, sir!" thundered the irate abbé. "Does monsieur think I am not a very busy man?"

Then softening a little, he said, with a smile:

"I won't come any more, my friend. I'll send my boots around to-morrow by my boy."

But the longest red-letter day has its ending, and time and tide beckon one with the brutality of an impatient jailer.

On my studio table is a well-stuffed envelope containing the documents relative to my impending exile—a stamped card of my identification, bearing the number of my cell, a plan of the slave-ship, and six red tags for my baggage.

The three pretty daughters of old Père Valois know of my approaching departure, and say cheering things to me as I pass the concierge's window.

Père Valois stands at the gate and stops me with: "Is it true, monsieur, you are going Saturday?"

"Yes," I answer; "unfortunately, it is quite true."

The old man sighs and replies: "I once had to leave Paris myself"; looking at me as if he were speaking to an old resident. "My regiment was ordered to the colonies. It was hard, monsieur, but I did my duty."

The morning of my sailing has arrived. The patron of the tobacco-shop, and madame his good wife, and the wine merchant, and the baker along the little street with its cobblestone-bed, have all wished me "bon voyage," accompanied with many handshakings. It is getting late and Père Valois has gone to hunt for a cab—a "galerie," as it is called, with a place for trunks on top. Twenty minutes go by, but no "galerie" is in sight. The three daughters of Père Valois run in different directions to find one, while I throw the remaining odds and ends in the studio into my valise. At last there is a sound of grating wheels below on the gravel court. The "galerie" has arrived—with the smallest of the three daughters inside, all out of breath from her run and terribly excited. There are the trunks and the valises and the bicycle in its crate to get down. Two soldiers, who have been calling on two of the daughters, come up to the studio and kindly offer their assistance. There is no time to lose, and in single file the procession starts down the atelier stairs, headed by Père Valois, who has just returned from his fruitless search considerably winded, and the three girls, the two red-trousered soldiers and myself tugging away at the rest of the baggage.

It is not often one departs with the assistance of three pretty femmes de ménage, a jolly old concierge, and a portion of the army of the French Republic. With many suggestions from my good friends and an assuring wave of the hand from the aged cocher, my luggage is roped and chained to the top of the rickety, little old cab, which sways and squeaks with the sudden weight, while the poor, small horse, upon whom has been devolved the task of making the 11.35 train, Gare St. Lazare, changes his position wearily from one leg to the other. He is evidently thinking out the distance, and has decided upon his gait.

"Bon voyage!" cry the three girls and Père Valois and the two soldiers, as the last trunk is chained on.

The dingy vehicle groans its way slowly out of the court. Just as it reaches the last gate it stops.

"What's the matter?" I ask, poking my head out of the window.

"Monsieur," says the aged cocher, "it is an impossibility! I regret very much to say that your bicycle will not pass through the gate."

A dozen heads in the windows above offer suggestions. I climb out and take a look; there are at least four inches to spare on either side in passing through the iron posts.

"Ah!" cries my cocher enthusiastically, "monsieur is right, happily for us!"

He cracks his whip, the little horse gathers itself together—a moment of careful driving and we are through and into the street and rumbling away, amid cheers from the windows above.

As I glance over my traps, I see a small bunch of roses tucked in the corner of my roll of rugs with an engraved card attached. "From Mademoiselle Ernestine Valois," it reads, and on the other side is written, in a small, fine hand, "Bon voyage."

I look back to bow my acknowledgment, but it is too late; we have turned the corner and the rue Vaugirard is but a memory!

*　　　*　　　*

*　　　*

But why go on telling you of what the little shops contain—how narrow and picturesque are the small streets—how gay the boulevards—what they do at the "Bullier"—or where they dine? It is Love that moves Paris—it is the motive power of this big, beautiful, polished city—the love of adventure, the love of intrigue, the love of being a bohemian if you will—but it is Love all the same!

"I work for love," hums the little couturière.

"I work for love," cries the miller of Marcel Legay.

"I live for love," sings the poet.

"For the love of art I am a painter," sighs Edmond, in his atelier—"and for her!"

"For the love of it I mold and model and create," chants the sculptor—"and for her!"

It is the Woman who dominates Paris—"Les petites femmes!" who have inspired its art through the skill of these artisans.

"Monsieur! monsieur! Please buy this fisherman doll!" cries a poor old woman outside of your train compartment, as you are leaving Havre for Paris.

"Monsieur!" screams a girl, running near the open window with a little fishergirl doll uplifted.

"What, you don't want it? You have bought one? Ah! I see," cries the pretty vendor; "but it is a boy doll—he will be sad if he goes to Paris without a companion!"

Take all the little fishergirls away from Paris—from the Quartier Latin—and you would find chaos and a morgue!

L'amour! that is it—L'amour!—L'amour!—L'amour!

www.ingramcontent.com/pod-product-compliance
Lightning Source LLC
Chambersburg PA
CBHW021201020426
42331CB00003B/164